SAFE
PEOPLE

Resources by Henry Cloud and John Townsend

Books

Boundaries (and workbook)
Boundaries in Dating (and workbook)
Boundaries in Marriage (and workbook)
Boundaries with Kids (and workbook)
Boundaries with Teens (Townsend)
Changes That Heal (and workbook) (Cloud)
Hiding from Love (Townsend)
How People Grow (and workbook)
How to Have That Difficult Conversation
Making Small Groups Work
Our Mothers, Ourselves (and workbook)
Raising Great Kids
Raising Great Kids Workbook for Parents of Preschoolers
Raising Great Kids Workbook for Parents of School-Age Children
Raising Great Kids Workbook for Parents of Teenagers
Safe People (and workbook)
The Entitlement Cure (Townsend)
12 "Christian" Beliefs That Can Drive You Crazy

Video Curriculum

Boundaries
Boundaries in Marriage
Boundaries with Kids

Audio

Boundaries
Boundaries in Dating
Boundaries in Marriage
Boundaries with Kids
Boundaries with Teens (Townsend)
Changes That Heal (Cloud)
How People Grow
Making Small Groups Work
Our Mothers, Ourselves
Raising Great Kids

HOW TO FIND RELATIONSHIPS
THAT ARE GOOD FOR YOU

SAFE
PEOPLE

and avoid those that aren't

DR. HENRY CLOUD *and* DR. JOHN TOWNSEND

ZONDERVAN®

ZONDERVAN

Safe People
Copyright © 1995 by Henry Cloud and John Townsend

Requests for information should be addressed to:
Zondervan, 3900 *Sparks Drive SE, Grand Rapids, Michigan 49546*

This edition: ISBN 978-0-310-34579-4 (softcover)
ISBN 978-0-310-26237-4 (audio)
ISBN 978-0-310-29814-4 (ebook)

Library of Congress Cataloging-in-Publication Data

Cloud, Henry
    Safe people: how to find relationships that are good for you and avoid those that aren't /
Henry Cloud and John Townsend
      p. cm.
     ISBN 978-0-310-21084-9 (softcover)
    1. Interpersonal relations—Religious aspects—Christianity 2. Christian Life I Townsend, John
Sims, 1952-. II. Title.
BV4597.52.C56 -1995
248.4—dc 20   95-7658

Published in association with Yates & Yates, www.yates2.com.

Interior design: Sherri L. Hoffman

First printing June 2016 / Printed in the United States of America

HB 03.02.2023

From Henry:
To Tori and my friends

From John:
To Barbi, my safest person

CONTENTS

Acknowledgments

WE WOULD LIKE to thank the following people:

the attendees of Monday Night Solutions in Irvine, California, who reacted to the early stages of the material in this book;

our partner, Bob Whiton, for his integrity and diligence;

our friend, Steve Tucker, for his heart for Jesus;

our agent, Sealy Yates, for his direction and support;

our editor, Sandy Vander Zicht, for her perseverance in the writing process.

INTRODUCTION

H AVE YOU EVER said any of the following things to yourself?

- How can I learn to pick better friends?
- Why do I choose people who let me down?
- How did I end up with this critical boss?
- How do I attract irresponsible people?
- Why did I invest money with that unscrupulous person?
- What is it about me that draws the wrong types to me?
- Why am I drawn to the wrong types?

If you have, then this book was written for you. It deals with the problem of character discernment, a skill that many of us lack. And yet the ability to determine good character in people is one of God's most vital ingredients for our personal and spiritual growth.

What is character discernment? It is simply being able to tell the "sheep from the goats" in your life, evaluating who is good for you, and who isn't. And those who are good for us we call "safe people," those individuals who truly make us better people by their presence in our lives.

Safe people are individuals who draw us closer to being the people God intended us to be. Though not perfect, they are "good enough" in their own character that the net effect of their presence in our lives is positive. They are accepting, honest, and present, and they help us bear good fruit in our lives.

As therapists, we have observed over the years one simple yet profound fact: We need each other. God designed us to be his hands and feet, to support, comfort, and encourage each other: "For where two or three come together in my name, there am I with them" (Matt. 18:20).

Many people act on that need and reach out for relationship. They reach out when they are lonely or stressed out. They reach out when they want someone to share their joys and successes. They

11

reach out when they need someone to understand their losses and problems. And they reach out when they need wisdom and guidance.

The problem is, we often pick the wrong people to trust. For many reasons, we will reach out to those who abandon, neglect, damage, or tear us down. Our blindness to who is good for us and who isn't can cause tragedies like depression, compulsive behaviors, marriage conflicts, and work problems. Sadly, your ability to pick out a good car may be better than your ability to pick good friendships.

But there is hope. We believe that the Bible contains the keys to understanding how to tell safe people from unsafe ones. It also teaches how to become safe people for others. In this age of broken relationships, these scriptural principles are both timeless and timely.

A Bird's-Eye View

Here is an outline of what this book will teach you about safe people.

In Part 1, "Unsafe People," you'll learn who unsafe people are and the twenty identifying traits of unsafe people (chapters 1–4).

In Part 2, "Do I Attract Unsafe People?" you'll get a picture of the origin of the problem: why you currently choose the wrong people, and how to repair this problem (chapters 5–8).

In Part 3, "Safe People," you will learn more about what safe people are and why you need them. You will also receive practical help on successfully meeting and relating to safe people.

We designed this book to help you look both outside *and* inside yourself. You will look *outside* yourself as you learn to stand back and critically evaluate the people in whom you are investing yourself. As you use the scriptural principles in this book, you will find that your eyes will become opened to the true nature of others, both good and bad.

Safe People will also help you look *inside* yourself. You will find your blind spots and vulnerabilities and understand why you are easy prey to manipulative people, or susceptible to controlling individuals. You'll gain important awareness of your weaknesses and learn how to mature past them. Also, you'll look inside and see the ways you yourself may be unsafe for others. God wants to help you expose those parts and mature in those areas.

A final word here: As you begin to educate yourself in this crucial area, remember that God understands the struggle to open up, to trust, and to love. Though he is God, he also gets hurt. He deeply desires to bring you into his world of relationship with him and with those who represent him. So as you read this guide to safe people, we pray that you will sense the impassioned concern of God for you in this area. "Being confident of this, that he who began a good work in you will carry it on to completion until the day of Christ Jesus" (Phil. 1:6).

HENRY CLOUD, PH.D.
JOHN TOWNSEND, PH.D.

PART ONE

Unsafe People

CHAPTER ONE

What Is an Unsafe Person?

A s a college student, I (John) dated around a bit, but I enjoyed casual friendships more. Until a friend introduced me to Karen. From the moment I saw her standing in my friend's living room, my world turned upside down.

Karen was an attractive blonde and a committed Christian, with a sly sense of humor that peeked out at unexpected intervals. Intelligent and popular, she was at home in both formal settings and at a Saturday touch football game.

We started dating, and our relationship quickly became exclusive. We dined at cheap student-friendly restaurants. We went out with friends. Sometimes we even studied together. One of our favorite activities was sitting in the campus center, making up stories about the people who walked by. She'd see an FBI agent on the prowl, and I'd add that the agent was actually part of a conspiracy to take the university president hostage.

Over the next few months, our relationship progressed. I was still dumbfounded at how fortunate I was to have Karen, and I thought that perhaps this was the woman God had meant for me to marry. Caught up in my wonder and excitement, however, I missed a few things. A few times Karen couldn't meet me for pizza or a class, and she'd say she was busy and quickly change the subject. I figured I probably "needed too much" from her and never pressed her on it.

One time I dropped by her apartment to surprise her. Hearing voices, I knocked, and said, "It's me." The voices stopped. After knocking several times, I shrugged and left. Maybe Karen and a girl-friend were having a private talk. *Who am I to intrude?* I thought.

Another time my friend Bill told me he'd heard that Karen had a history of breaking hearts. "Be careful," he said. Certain that Bill was probably jealous or mistaken, I brushed it off.

But most troubling was what we'd do when we were together. When it was what Karen wanted, it was a pleasure. If she needed to hit the books, she made it fun. If it was time to play, she was a riot. But if it was I who needed to study, instead of studying with me she'd get impatient and go out with her friends.

The same imbalance occurred on a deeper level. I was mostly "there" for her; she seldom was for me. Once, when I was in the mid-dle of a conflict with a friend, Karen didn't see me for a few days to "let me sort it out."

One day the truth I'd been avoiding came crashing down on me. I walked into her apartment and caught her kissing another guy.

I remember Karen looking around to see me, a surprised expres-sion on her face. She broke her clutch with my replacement. Then, holding his hand, she smiled and said to me, "I've been meaning to tell you, John, but I knew you'd be the kind of guy who understands."

And I did, in a way. No temper tantrum. I didn't jerk Mr. New's head off, or challenge him to a duel. True to form in my relationship with Karen, I smiled in a hurt-but-mature way, and mumbled some-thing like, "Absolutely, I understand. I'm sure it was hard for you."

Karen thanked me for this gift of "understanding," and I walked away.

I saw her occasionally over the next few months, but our lives began moving in different directions. I took longer than a few months to recover, however. I'd thought Karen and I were much more involved than we were, and I was in shock. I'd talked about thoughts and feelings that no one else was privy to and entrusted her with deep parts of me. I was under the impression that our souls were becoming deeply intertwined in preparation for a lifetime of love, family, fun, and service to God and others.

It took a long time for me to accept the fact that Karen could switch beaus like most of us change socks. In fact, I heard through the grapevine that this scenario repeated itself many times. The rela-tionship hurt my pride and my sense of trust. But even more, I began doubting myself.

What's really funny is that even though I knew how bad Karen was for me, the "catch my breath" feeling didn't go away for a long time. I'd pray about her; friends would counsel me and listen to my grief. I'd see all the character flaws I'd missed: Duplicity. Dishonesty. Irresponsibility. Self-centeredness.

And then I'd see a snapshot of her. Or, even worse, catch her walking down a hall. And I'd be flooded with tender, longing aches that were just as strong as the day we'd met. You could have been walking with me, reading out loud a long list of Karen's Seven Deadly Sins, and it wouldn't have mattered. I'd still be suffering from cardiac flip-flops.

Well, God was good to me, and I grew up in some areas. I finally did marry, and Barbi and I are very much in love. I can't imagine life without her. And I can see all the reasons Karen and I wouldn't have worked out. Yet for years I wondered why I could be so wrong about thinking someone so wrong was so right.

Is This Your Life?

Now, let's move out of the romantic sphere into all of your relationships. Think for a minute. Have you ever had a relationship with a Karen? Maybe a best friend. A coworker. A relative or church acquaintance. Have you had more than one?

Most of us have. Have you ever been left, used, or hurt? And asked yourself, *What in the world am I doing wrong?* You're not alone.

When we're wounded by people, it's second nature to blame our need for attachment. You may think, *There I go again, trusting people and not God,* or *Just goes to show you, people can't be depended on.*

Though it's true that people aren't perfect lovers the way God is, Scripture teaches that God created us for relationship with both him and with each other. When at Creation God declared, "It is not good for the man to be alone" (Gen. 2:18), he was not just talking about marriage. He was declaring the importance of relationships. Part of being made in God's image is having a need to be in relationship.

The problem isn't our need for friendship and connection. That's good, a God-ordained need that he built inside us. But without the proper maturity and skills, that need for support and attachment can get us into real trouble. The real problem is that we are untrained in discerning the character of people.

Character Discernment

One evening I (Henry) spoke to a group of Christian college students about dating and relationships. At the close of the talk, I asked, "What qualities do you look for in a potential date or mate?" The answers went something like this: "I want someone spiritual, godly, ambitious, fun to be with," and so on. They replied as I had expected. And that disturbed me, for as a counselor and as a person, I know that these are not the issues that cause relationships to break apart.

When I questioned the audience a bit further, asking them about character and relational issues, they were in the dark. They continued to give me broad religious answers and descriptions of people that had little to do with what the Bible actually says about relationships.

People in trouble don't say broad religious issues are the problem. They say:

- He doesn't listen to me.
- She is so perfect that she can't understand my struggles.
- He seems so distant that I feel alone.
- She always tries to control me.
- He makes promises but really doesn't follow through.
- He is condemning and judgmental.
- She is always angry at me for something I did or didn't do.
- I tend to be my worst self with him or her.
- I cannot trust him.

And the list could go on. These are the painful complaints that friends and counselors hear from hurting people as they describe their relationships.

When we listen to God address his problem relationships, the list is much more like the second than the first. He says that, among other things, his people are "far away" (Isa. 29:13), "unfaithful" (Josh. 22:16), "proud and perfectionistic" (Deut. 8:14; Ps. 36:2), "unloving" (1 John 4:20), and "judgmental" (Rom. 2:1).

God does not use religious terms and language when he discusses people. He talks about how people treat him and others, and whether or not they get things done as they said they would. In short, he looks at someone's *character.* He is looking at their makeup as a person and the way that that character interacts with him and the world. The Bible is full of "religious" people who could have fulfilled the list the students gave that night. But these people are the ones that Jesus and the Old Testament prophets confronted over and over. They look good on the outside or from a distance, but to get close to them is a nightmare.

We do not get a lot of training in evaluating character. We tend to look on the outside and not the inside of a person (1 Sam. 16:7; Matt. 23:25–28). *So we choose people based on outward appearance, and then experience the inside of them.* We look at worldly success, charm, looks, humor, status and education, accomplishments, talents and giftedness, or religious activity. But then we experience the pain of being in a real relationship with them, and come up very empty-handed.

Who Are the Bad Guys?

My (John's) boys love Saturday morning cartoons. They especially like the superhero-supervillain types, and they enjoy picking out which character is the good guy and which is the bad guy. These shows, of course, make it easy for them: the good guys are clean-cut with heroic features and strong voices. But the bad guys are ugly, dress horribly, and have low, menacing voices.

In real life, the bad guys aren't that easy to pick out. Unsafe people are particularly difficult to spot. Quite often, unsafe people appear winsome and promising, and their character problems are often subtle. So how do we know whom to trust?

While there are many different kinds of unsafe people, many of them fall under three categories: the abandoners, the critics, and the irresponsibles.

Abandoners

Abandoners are people who can start a relationship, but who can't finish it.

Ron had recently come to the painful conclusion that, at thirty-nine, he had no significant friendships that had lasted over one year.

"You know, I'll be forty soon," he confided, "and I'd always thought that by that milestone, I'd have several 'anchors': men I'd known for at least a decade, men with whom I'd spend time praying, playing golf, arguing, and trusting with my deepest feelings.

"It hasn't happened yet. I'll meet a guy, we'll get together for lunch, meet the wives, and within a few months, they've lost my number. My slogan for them is, 'Nice guys—where'd they go?'"

Ron was drawn to abandoners. People who can start a relationship—but can't finish it. They begin with statements about companionship and commitment, but they leave us when we need them most.

Often, abandoners have been abandoned themselves. Sometimes, afraid of true closeness, they prefer shallow acquaintances. Others are looking for perfect friends, and they leave when the cracks start showing.

Abandoners destroy trust. Those they leave in their wake are apt to say, "I'll never have anyone who will be there for me." This is a far cry from God's ideal, that we be "rooted and established in love" (Eph. 3:17). And those who continually pick abandoners often become depressed, develop compulsive behaviors, or worse.

Critics

Critics are people who take a parental role with everyone they know. They are judgmental, speak the truth without love, and have no room for grace or forgiveness.

Martha walked out of the church, shaking her head. It was *déjà vu* all over again! She'd been searching for a safe fellowship of Christians where she could grow and serve. For the last year, she'd spent several weeks at various churches, getting to know the attitudes and values of the congregation.

It was uncanny. The last three churches she'd visited were legalistic, rigid, and critical. Their doctrine could be summarized, "If you're a Christian, you should have your act together." And she'd done it again. She'd sat through a sermon on how godly Christians don't sin, and ungodly ones do.

Even though Martha understood that all of us sin, whether we are Christians or not, she couldn't shake her real worry. *Why was I attracted to this type again? What's wrong with me?*

Critics are more concerned with confronting errors than they are with making connections. For example, they often jump on doctrinal and ethical bandwagons (which are important) and neglect issues of love, compassion, and forgiveness. They often confuse weakness with sinfulness, and therefore condemn others when they have problems.

Critics tend to point the finger outside, rather than at themselves. They will sometimes become indignant at the trouble others cause, and propose solutions like "think, feel, believe, and act like my group" as the cure-all.

Critics often deeply love truth and righteousness. Because they are clear thinkers, they can be good people to go to for information. But don't go to them for relationship, for their truth often comes poisoned with judgmentalism.

If you're attracted to critical people, you may find relief in their clarity of thought and purity of vision. But you'll also find yourself guilt-ridden, compliant, and unable to make mistakes without tremendous anxiety.

Irresponsibles

Irresponsibles are people who don't take care of themselves or others. They have problems with delaying gratification, they don't consider the consequences of their actions, and they don't follow through on their commitments. They are like grown-up children.

Jeremy, a friend of mine (John's), was constantly in financial straits. He was always broke and in a money crisis. He would come to me and ask for a loan, saying, "I'll pay you back in a few weeks, when things straighten out."

I cared a lot for Jeremy and felt valued that he trusted me enough to ask. So I'd lend him the money. Time would pass, there would be no repayment, and he wouldn't mention it. Then, months later, he'd be in another jam and ask for help again. I'd grudgingly agree, he'd promise to pay both loans back, and again, nothing would happen.

Finally, I figured out what to do. I told Jeremy, "From now on, the word *loan* doesn't exist between us: only *gift*. I know you mean to pay me back, but you don't change your financial habits enough to pull it off. So when you ask for help, I'll either give you a gift, never expecting to see the money again, or I'll just say no to the request."

Jeremy thought I was crazy, but it helped me a lot. That's the kind of thinking you have to have to survive with irresponsibles. If you depend on them to do what they say, you can end up in financial, functional, and emotional trouble.

If you're drawn to irresponsible people, you may be doing the following:

You pick up after them.
You apologize to others for them.
You make excuses for them.
You give them chance after chance after chance.
You pay for their sins and forgetfulness.
You nag them.
You resent them.

Many irresponsibles are caring, warm, fun-loving people. I like irresponsibles. They help me notice what's going on in life today instead of being anxious about tomorrow. There isn't a place in their head for tomorrow! They're often empathic and understanding. But while I like irresponsibles, I just don't trust them. The irresponsible's lack of dependability can cause us many problems, ranging from making us wait for her at a restaurant to losing a crucial business deal because he didn't get the documentation in on time. As Proverbs puts it: "Better to meet a bear robbed of her cubs than a fool in his folly" (17:12).

Because the irresponsible has problems in delaying gratification, he or she often becomes alcoholic, addicted to sexual gratification, and in debt.

You may be providing a safety net for an irresponsible. For some reason, you end up paying for his or her problems. We could be talking about a friend, an adult child, a spouse, or a business relationship. For every irresponsible, there is an enabler, someone who protects them.

These are just three examples of the many types of unsafe people. Think about your present support system. You may be in a relationship with an abandoner, a critic, or an irresponsible.

In the following chapters, we will talk about more specific character traits of unsafe people. And we will contrast them with the godly character traits that safe people have. In this way you will be able to look for danger signals in your relationships—then learn to make wise decisions about how to handle the unsafe people in *your* life.

CHAPTER TWO

Personal Traits of Unsafe People

MARY AND DONNA were partners in a successful decorating firm. Over the years, they had "been there" for one another in many difficult times. But one day Mary confronted Donna on a behavior that had been bothering her. "You always interrupt me when we are meeting with clients," she said. "It makes me feel inferior."

"Well, maybe you are!" Donna shot back.

Mary stared at her, stunned. "How can you say that?" she asked. "We're partners! I've always worked just as hard as you."

But Donna could not take the implication that she was not perfect. Unable to hear or even consider the message, she attacked the messenger. When Mary tried to resolve the conflict, her friend ended the relationship and the association.

Mary was devastated. But as she thought back over the years with Donna, she remembered seeing her friend do the same thing with other people. If Donna did not get her way, she would turn on the other person with a judgmental vengeance and literally write that person out of her life. Long before Donna dropped Mary, there were signs that she was an unsafe person. (Mary also needed to look more carefully at how she chose her friends, because she had run into this kind of rejection before. But we'll talk about our own responsibility for getting into unsafe relationships in chapter 5.)

Unsafe people have personal traits that make them extremely dangerous to other people. They act as if they "have it all together." They are self-righteous. They demand trust. And when their facade of perfection is stripped away, they blow up, like Donna, or disappear.

As you read through the next two chapters, you will learn about twenty traits of unsafe people. This chapter describes eleven personal traits of unsafe people; the next chapter details nine interpersonal traits of unsafe people. These traits are warning signals, and if you observe them in any of your relationships, you should proceed in that relationship with caution and much prayer.

This chapter and the next can teach you much by "negative example." For every negative trait mentioned, there is a corresponding positive one. Look at the positive trait, and you will have a good working definition of a safe person. Safe people, for example, admit their weaknesses. They are humble. And they prove their trustworthiness over time. Keep these positive traits in mind when you read Part 3: "Safe People." And watch for these traits in your relationships as well. As you learn about these twenty traits, you will hone your character discernment skills and learn to distinguish the safe from the unsafe.

1. **Unsafe people think they "have it all together" instead of admitting their weaknesses.**

Over lunch one day, my friend Sally described a friendship to me. "I really love and admire Julia, but . . ." she sighed. "Something's just not right with our friendship."

"What do you mean?" I (Henry) asked.

"I guess it is that she doesn't have any needs," Sally explained. "I feel like I am always the one with the problems. I talk about problems in my marriage and in the rest of my life, and get really vulnerable, but she never does. She seems to have it all together, and I feel like the totally weak one."

"What is it about this that bothers you the most?" I asked.

"I guess it is that I do not feel like she needs me," she said.

When someone "has it all together," that person's friends will suffer these predictable results:

- *Feeling disconnected.* Intimacy is built on sharing weaknesses, and friendship involves sharing vulnerabilities.
- *Feeling "one down."* There is an implied superiority in the one that has no need for the other.
- *Feeling weaker than one actually is.* The vulnerable one plays the "weakness" role in the relationship. There is no balance, for she is not allowed to be strong.

- *Feeling dependent on the "strong one."* The weaker one thinks she needs the stronger one to survive.
- *Feeling anger and hostility at the "together" one.* The vulnerable person grows tired of the "together" facade of the stronger person.
- *Feeling the need to compete to reverse the role.* The weaker person feels stuck in her role and fights to change it.

The "weak" one may try to be the "strong" one in some other relationships to compensate for her lack of strength in this relationship. Instead of suffering through only one bad relationship, she may end up with several unbalanced, unsafe relationships. She would do better to balance elements of strength and weakness in each of her relationships.

This pattern also keeps the "strong" one from growing spiritually and emotionally. We grow in part by confessing our faults and weaknesses to each other (James 5:16; Eccl. 4:10). If we are always being strong and without needs, we are not growing, and we are setting ourselves up for a very dangerous fall.

2. Unsafe people are religious instead of spiritual.

I remember when I (Henry) first became a committed Christian. For a long time, I really looked up to people who were religious. I admired their dedication to God and their Bible knowledge. They seemed so strong and "together" that I wanted to be like them.

For about five years, I hung around these kinds of people. During that time I grew a lot and learned a lot of theology, but unknowingly, I also was getting farther and farther away from being a real person. I became more and more "religious," and less and less of what I now understand to be spiritual. I was losing touch with my vulnerability, my pain, my need for other people, my sinfulness and "bad parts," and many other aspects of what it means to be a person.

The wake-up call came when I had a series of failed relationships. I had to begin to look at why I could not get close to people and trust them at a very deep level, and why I knew more and more about God but felt farther and farther away from him.

My graduate school training required some therapy, so when I got into a group where people were real, they started confronting me in the areas where I was faking it. I learned to open up about my

pain and inadequacies, and I got closer to others as I was more vulnerable and needed them more. As the safe people around me loved
me just like I was, I learned to open up about my struggles, sinfulness, and imperfections. And I started to really grow as a person and
learned a lot more about God than I had known when I had been so
"religious."

After that, I was able to recognize people who weren't "real,"
although they seemed very spiritual. And I found that I was able to
pick better friends, people who really knew God and his ways
instead of a lot of religious language and activities, truly relational
people who were able to understand and love others and were honest about themselves and about life.

3. Unsafe people are defensive instead of open to feedback.

I was organizing a conference with a colleague I'll call Jay. We
each had different responsibilities. Jay was responsible for securing
the site, for making sure an overhead projector and flip chart were
available, and for shipping books to the workshop.

The night before the event, Jay called me. "Do you have any
extra copies of your books you could bring along?"

"What do you mean?" I asked.

"I thought it would be good to sell your books at the workshop."

"But you were supposed to take care of that!" I replied.

"I had too many things to do," he said.

Trying with all my might to hang on to my patience, I said,
"But we agreed that shipping books to the conference was *your*
responsibility."

"You always concentrate on the things that go wrong," he said
angrily. "You never tell me about the things that I do right. Who are
you to say that you always do things right?"

Jay is an example of a unsafe person. When I confronted him on
his lack of responsibility, he became defensive and started making
excuses and attacking me.

The conversation with Jay was in marked contrast to a phone
call I had had a couple of weeks before with a friend. That day my
heart pounded as I picked up the phone to call a friend. I had
noticed some things about him that troubled me, and I knew he
needed to be confronted, but I knew that our relationship could suffer if he didn't take it well.

I expected him to be very defensive and hurt. But to my surprise he said, "Really? Tell me how I do that."

I proceeded to explain to him why I thought what he was doing was destructive. "Gosh," he said, "I never thought about that. But I can see what you are saying—it's certainly a weakness of mine. Can you help me to get out of that pattern?"

I was really relieved to hear his openness, and of course I agreed to help. But at a deeper level, I felt closer to him and very respectful of his response. I could see that he was more interested in doing what was right than appearing "right" in his own eyes.

This is one of the marks of a truly safe person: they are confrontable. Every relationship has problems, because every person has problems, and the place that our problems appear most glaringly is in our close relationships. The key is whether or not we can hear from others where we are wrong, and accept their feedback without getting defensive. Time and again, the Bible says that someone who listens to feedback from others is wise, but someone who does not is a fool. As Proverbs 9:7–9 says: "Whoever corrects a mocker invites insult; whoever rebukes a wicked man incurs abuse. Do not rebuke a mocker or he will hate you; rebuke a wise man and he will love you. Instruct a wise man and he will be wiser still; teach a righteous man and he will add to his learning."

The Bible is clear about the need to be able to hear rebuke from others (Matt. 18:15). Confrontation helps us learn about ourselves and change destructive patterns.

All close relationships hurt, because no perfect people live on the earth. But the safe people are the wise ones that can hear their sin and respond to our hurt. In short, they can "own" where they are wrong. If, however, someone has the character trait of defensiveness, when we need to confront him, we are going to be stuck with all the hurt that his natural imperfections cause in the relationship. Someone who does not own his need to change does not change, and the hurt is likely to continue.

4. Unsafe people are self-righteous instead of humble.

The Pharisees of Jesus' time were notorious for taking pride in their own righteousness. In fact, Jesus told a parable that poked fun of their attitude:

> Two men went up to the temple to pray, one a Pharisee and the other a tax collector. The Pharisee stood up and prayed about himself: "God, I thank you that I am not like other men—robbers, evildoers, adulterers—or even like this tax collector. I fast twice a week and give a tenth of all I get."
>
> But the tax collector stood at a distance. He would not even look up to heaven, but beat his breast and said, "God, have mercy on me, a sinner."
>
> I tell you that this man, rather than the other, went home justified before God.
>
> (LUKE 18:10–14)

The tax gatherer did not see himself as righteous. Instead, he sought grace humbly, for he knew that only through God's grace could he be loved and accepted. The Pharisee, however, saw *himself* as good, and *others* as bad. He believed—wrongly—that all "badness" was outside of himself.

Unsafe people will never identify with others as fellow sinners and strugglers, because they see themselves as somehow "above all of that." This "I'm better than you" dynamic produces a lot of shame and guilt in people who are associated with this type of unsafe person. It significantly blocks intimacy because the two people are never on "even ground," which is where human intimacy takes place. It sets up comparison, competitive strivings, defensiveness, and alienation.

Psychologists call this dynamic a "not me" experience: People have a character structure that does not allow them to see certain realities as part of themselves. They project things onto others and cannot own their own flaws. Unfortunately, many Christians have this mentality about sin in general. They will talk about the people "in the world," as if they are somehow not able to identify with them.

5. Unsafe people only apologize instead of changing their behavior.

"But he's really sorry this time," she said. "When I confronted him with what I knew, he cried and said he was so heartbroken about what he had done. I could tell he was really torn up about it."

My counselee was referring to her husband, whom she had discovered had been seeing another woman. She was being taken in by his "true pain" over what he had done and his promises never to do it again. However, he had made similar "confessions" countless times before. Each time, he was "so sorry." He cried and made very short-lived 180-degree turnarounds. This was the fourth time that he had been involved with another woman. And each previous time, he had been "sorry."

The truth is, however, that sorry is as sorry does. The Bible's word for this is *repentance*, and it means a true turnaround. But unlike the "spins" that this man had made, a true turnaround is one that lasts. That does not mean that there is perfect behavior after that point, but that the change is real and that it bears fruit over time.

To repent means to change one's mind and to turn around and be transformed. Before Jesus' ministry began, John the Baptist sternly preached repentance to the Jews: "You brood of vipers! Who warned you to flee from the coming wrath? *Produce fruit in keeping with repentance.*... The ax is already at the root of the trees, and every tree that does not produce good fruit will be cut down and thrown into the fire" (Luke 3:7–9, emphasis mine).

A wife of a well-known Christian leader once said to me, "I cannot remember in twenty-five years of marriage that I have mentioned something hurtful that my husband did that he ever did again. When he says he is sorry, he means it, and he changes." What a testimony that was!

Repentant people will recognize a wrong and really want to change because they do not want to be that kind of person. They are motivated by love to not hurt anyone like that again. These are trustworthy people because they are on the road to holiness and change, and their behavior matters to them.

People who apologize quickly may act like they are sorry or as if they are interested in holiness, but they are really leading someone on. They may say all the words, and some are taken in by their tears and "sorrow." But in reality they are more sorry about getting caught. They do not change, and the future will be exactly like the past.

Again, the issue here is not perfection. People who are changing still are not perfect and may sin again. But there is a qualitative change that is visible in people of repentance that does not have to do with guilt, getting caught, or trying to get someone off their back.

The prognosis for change is always better when it is not motivated by a "getting caught" episode, but by real confession and coming to the light about what is wrong. Sometimes, when someone is "caught," he will repent and change, but that repentance can only be tested over time.

The general principle is to look for whether the "repentance" is motivated from outside pressure or from true internal desire to change. Getting caught or adapting to someone's anger is not a long-lasting motivator. Eventually the motivations must be a hunger and thirst for righteousness and love for the injured.

6. **Unsafe people avoid working on their problems instead of dealing with them.**

Many people are familiar with the Twelve Steps of the recovery movement. Using these steps, people suffering from addictions work through their problems, and in a systematic way; they begin to develop character.

Unsafe people, however, resist any form of character growth or maturation. Unsafe people

do not admit that they have problems, or they think they can solve the problems by themselves.

do not submit their life and will to God.

do not confess when they have wronged someone.

do not forgive people who have hurt them.

avoid facing relationship problems directly and openly.

do not hunger and thirst for righteousness.

treat others with a lack of empathy.

are not open to confrontation from others.

are not in a process of learning and growing.

do not take responsibility for their lives.

blame other people for their problems.

do not want to share their problems with others to help them grow.

People who are uninvolved in character growth can be unsafe, because they are shut off from awareness of their own problems and God's resources to transform those problems. Instead, they act out of their unconscious hurts, and then hurt others.

7. Unsafe people demand trust, instead of earning it.

The husband who demanded trust from his wife after an affair is a glaring example of someone who feels entitled to trust. But there are other examples that are not so glaring. I knew a man named Donald who demanded trust from his boss. When Donald's boss asked him to account for his work hours, Donald got so offended that he quit the company and complained to others about the "offense."

Some people feel that they are entitled to trust. We often hear of someone saying, "So you don't trust me." Or "Are you questioning my integrity?" Or "You don't believe me." They get defensive and angry because someone questions their actions, and they think they are above being questioned or having to prove their trustworthiness. But none of us is above questioning, and to take offense at it is very prideful.

Even the most trustworthy man of all time—Jesus himself—did not demand blind trust. He told the Jews who were challenging him, "Do not believe me unless I do what my Father does. But if I do it, even though you do not believe me, believe the miracles, that you may learn and understand that the Father is in me, and I in the Father" (John 10:37–38). In other words, Jesus told them to test what he said by his actions; his miracles proved his words to be true.

If, like Jesus, we are truly trustworthy, we would welcome questioning from our loved ones on our "trustability." We would want others to see our deeds and actions so that they would feel more comfortable. We would want to know what gives them suspicion or fear and try to do everything to allay those fears. Above all, we want to make people feel comfortable with us.

In a sense, we should always be open to an "audit" from the ones we care about. If we are truly serious about growing, we want to know if we are unknowingly doing something wrong (Ps. 139:23–24). Hidden sins and problems are destructive to us, and if we long to grow, we would want them exposed and healed.

We will often get questions in seminars from a spouse who has done something wrong but is angry because his or her spouse won't "trust me even though I have said I'm sorry." They have to be confronted and reminded that trust has to be earned and trustworthiness has to be demonstrated over time. It is a sad commentary that some husbands and wives are more disturbed by the fact that their spouse won't trust them than they are at whatever they had done to create that level of mistrust.

In short, we are not in any way "entitled" to perfect opinions of us by others. Those opinions are earned. Be wary of people who say, "How dare you question my integrity!"

8. **Unsafe people believe they are perfect instead of admitting their faults.**

Unsafe people are on a mission to prove that they are perfect. Using their work, family, abilities, or religion, they try to project an image of perfection, and their image becomes more important to them than the relationships they are in. If someone threatens their image, they will attack that person, for they must keep up their image at all costs.

Love, however, depends in part on our ability to own and share our faults. The one who is forgiven much, loves much (Luke 7:47). "Perfect" people cannot internalize grace, so they will not feel loved at a deep level. Therefore, as Jesus pointed out, they do not have a lot of love to give to others. All they have is their "perfection," and that is pretty shallow and not very nourishing. In addition, relationships with perfect people are very hurtful, because they dodge any "badness" that appears in the relationship. They will fight, blame, and point fingers—anything that will put the badness onto the other person so that they can remain blameless.

9. **Unsafe people blame others instead of taking responsibility.**

Safe people take responsibility for their lives. Unsafe people don't. When we become aware of our problems and character issues, God holds us responsible for dealing with them and facing the tough changes that we have to make. Instead of doing this, however, unsafe people will often choose to blame other people, their past, God, sin, or anything else they can find. This tendency to blame others first appeared in Adam and Eve (Gen. 3:12–13), and we have continued it to this day. It is called externalizing our problems.

In other words, we give the responsibility of whatever we are saddled with away to some outside agent.

"I did it because I had to."

"I had no choice."

"I can't change because my mother abandoned me when I was five."

"You are ruining my life."

"God has it in for me."

And on and on.

If I walk out of my office today and get hit by a drunk driver, that will not be my fault. But it will be my responsibility to deal with the outcome. I am the one who has to go to the doctor and get surgery. I am the one who will have to go to the physical therapist. I am the one who will have to grieve. And I will be the one who has to work through the anger and do the forgiving. *Those things are all my responsibility, even though I did not choose to get hit by a drunk driver.*

Unsafe people do not do that hard work. They stay angry, stuck, and bitter, sometimes for life. When they feel upset, they see others as the cause, and others as the ones who have to do all the changing. When they are abused, they hold on to it with a vengeance and spew hatred for the rest of their lives. When they are hurt, they wear it like a badge. And worst of all, when they are wrong, they blame it on others.

Denial is the active process that someone uses to avoid responsibility. It is different from being unaware of sin. When we are unaware, we do not know about our sin. Denial is more active than that. It is a style and an agenda, and it can be very aggressive when truth comes close. People with a style of denial and blaming are definitely on the list of unsafe people to avoid.

10. Unsafe people lie instead of telling the truth.

In a relationship, honesty is the bedrock foundation of a safe relationship. To the degree that there is deception, there is danger. Often we have heard spouses and friends talk about someone that they "thought they knew," only to find out that this person was living a whole other life they did not know about.

I was talking to a friend yesterday whose entire well-being in finances is gone now because he was deceived in a business relationship. He invested the majority of his money with a con artist.

And there are many whose emotional and spiritual security has been wiped out for the same reason. They invested all they had with someone who was deceiving them and found out that their relationship, or their family, or their faith was built on smoke and mirrors. They trusted someone's love to be real, and found out that the person was deceiving them all along to get things from them.

We are all deceivers to some degree. The difference between safe and unsafe "liars" is that safe people own their lies and see them as a problem to change as they become aware of their deception. Lying gives way to truth, confrontation, humility, and repentance. Unsafe people see deception as a strategy to cling to and to manage life and relationships. They defend instead of give up their lies. And there is no way a relationship can prosper and grow if one person is a liar.

11. Unsafe people are stagnant instead of growing.

Each of us has both fixed aspects of our character and things that we can change. For example, a naturally aggressive person will probably not change to be naturally passive. But that person can learn to channel that aggression in acceptable ways. This kind of change is part of the sanctification process that we undergo as we place ourselves under the lordship of Christ.

Safe people know that they are subject to change. They want to mature and grow over time. But unsafe people do not see their own problems; they are rigidly fixed and not subject to growth (Prov. 17:10). These people can be dangerous, and they will only change when there are enough limits placed on them that they are forced into great pain, humility, and loss. Without this confrontation, unsafe people will remain defiant and unchanged.

Reminder

One of the things that we want to emphasize throughout this book is that no one is perfect. Safe people will at times stumble and be "unsafe" for, after all, they are sinners too. So do not expect perfection.

Instead, when you are measuring someone's character, look at these traits in terms of degree. Everyone lies at some time or in some way. But not everyone is a pathological liar. Look for degrees of imperfection. If a person seems willing to change, forgive him graciously and work with him. But if he resists you, proceed with caution.

CHAPTER THREE

Interpersonal Traits of Unsafe People

ALBERT EINSTEIN'S WIDOW was being interviewed about her husband. One reporter asked her if she understood his theory of relativity. She replied, "I don't know Einstein's theory. But I know Einstein."

Mrs. Einstein "knew" her husband in a way no one else did: she was in relationship with him. In the same way, we can learn a great deal about who is safe by how they are in relationship with us.

In the last chapter, we learned about the eleven personal traits of unsafe people. In this chapter, we look at nine interpersonal traits of unsafe people. While personal traits describe "who we are," interpersonal traits describe "how we connect." These interpersonal traits are about how people operate in relationships, how they move close or pull away, and how they build up or destroy.

Use this chapter to help you examine the people in your life. As you observe them through the grid of these nine traits, you will begin to see the difference between the safe and unsafe people in your life.

1. Unsafe people avoid closeness instead of connecting.

We were created for intimacy, to connect with someone with heart, soul, and mind. Intimacy occurs when we are open, vulnerable, and honest, for these qualities help us to be close to each other. We know each other at deep levels when we share our real feelings, fears, failures, and hurts. This kind of sharing helps us to feel that we are not alone in the world. We are meant to have intimacy with

God and with people. If we do not, we experience isolation, even if we are in some kind of relationship.

Time with someone does not a connection make. Only true sharing and intimacy create connection. You need to question long-term relationships in which you do not get to know the other person. If you spend significant amounts of time with an individual and still feel far away from him or her, something is wrong. You do not have a connection that is nourishing to the soul. Furthermore, this can be a signal that real danger is present. People who are not able to get close often act out that isolation in affairs, two-faced betrayals, broken confidences and trusts, addictions, and a whole host of other problem dynamics.

Many marriages have this dynamic at work. Like a silent killer, this lack of intimacy eats away at the foundation of the relationship. Because there are no overt problems, nothing is said. Things are "fine." But then one spouse discovers that the other one is having an affair, or has an addiction that surprises everyone. When this happens, the external structure of the relationship—the one everyone thought was so good—breaks down.

Usually spouses know deep inside that things weren't really all that good. They had a nagging feeling of disconnection, but they did not know exactly what to do about it. So they continued to go along the same direction in life, until the catastrophe brought everything tumbling down.

Wayne, a friend of mine at church, had this effect on me. He was a pleasant enough fellow. We'd talk, go out with our wives, and have occasional lunches. He always seemed interested and caring. But something wasn't there.

I couldn't put words on my nagging doubt for the longest time. Finally, one day we were talking over lunch, and I noticed for the first time that Wayne never, ever discussed his deeper issues. His struggles. His pains. His failures. And he had no idea what to do about mine.

Wayne was quite bright and very interested in theology and spiritual matters. But there was a vacuum in the "inner parts" of our relationship. When I'd bring up a problem in my life, or express sadness or fear, Wayne would simply go away.

It was a little eerie. I'd be sharing something personal, then lob the conversational ball over to Wayne. And he'd look blank, be quiet, and then start talking about something else. He wasn't being hostile at all. He just had no place in his head for the deeper connection.

One night I received a call from his wife. She told me Wayne had been a closet addict of prescription pills for years, and tonight was having an adverse drug reaction. I arranged the emergency help he needed and got him into treatment.

Wayne's addiction wasn't a huge surprise to me. In fact, it helped answer some questions for me. Apparently, he handled all his feelings, needs, and relational struggles through drugs. He wasn't a "bad guy"—just someone who had no ability to be intimate.

If you are uneasy about a relationship, ask yourself, *Does this relationship breed more togetherness or more isolation within me?* If you feel alone in the relationship, that's not a good sign. But remember: the first person to look at is yourself. Your sense of detachment may be from some block inside of *you*. Sometimes our own fears and conflicts make it difficult for us to feel connected to someone. The problem can be ours. It can be theirs. And it can be both.

2. Unsafe people are only concerned about "I" instead of "we."

I met Barry, another Christian therapist, at a convention. We seemed to have a lot in common: values, professional interests, and the like. And my wife liked his wife. So we tried to spend some time together.

Things changed after a few engagements. Although we had a lot to talk about, I found myself dreading upcoming events with Barry. I'd think of ways to avoid him, get out of the appointment, or cut our time short.

I really berated myself for this. Thinking that I was just being selfish, I forced myself to spend time with him, thinking the extra time would increase our connection.

It didn't work. More and more, I dreaded seeing Barry. My stomach would literally get upset when I said yes to another evening with him.

One night I was on the phone with Barry, and I had to cut the conversation short. I was leaving town the next day, and my family needed some attention. It was a little awkward, because he was in the middle of a story about himself and a friend at work. But I said, "I need to get back to you on this. I've got to go and be with my family."

But Barry continued his story, at the same pace, not even drawing a breath. It was as if I'd said, "Please, go on."

I figured I hadn't been clear enough. I said, "Barry, gotta go." He didn't miss a lick, saying, "So I figured it was time to shop for a new car."

I was getting a little angry. The family was waiting in the family room for me to read stories. So I moved from words to actions. I said, "Barry, I'm hanging up now."

Apparently he didn't believe it, because as the receiver was leaving my ear, I could faintly hear him say, "Yeah, I've got a big weekend coming up . . ."

The relationship had its problems after that, as I learned he was hurt by my abruptness. But I just didn't have time for him to wind down. What's more, I wasn't sure if Barry even had the ability to wind down.

Barry was a nice guy. But I realized we weren't connecting. What I had thought was a relationship was actually Barry simply talking to himself; I served as an audience to Barry's conversation with himself. What an empty experience!

If unsafe people are self-centered, safe people are relationship-centered. And that priority shows itself in the all-important action of empathy.

Safe people are empathic.

A genuine connection is a mutual give-and-take of caring that flows between individuals. Both people bring their lives, loves, joys, and sorrows to the connection. Each brings her needs — yet has a deep interest in the life of the other person.

In safe relationships, empathy is a large part of the equation. We literally "enter the other person's head" and attempt to understand how he feels, what he believes, and how he thinks. Empathy is walking in the moccasins of another person, and not judging him until we can see what suffering he's been through to get to the point he's at.

Empathy is not easy. It involves letting go of your opinion and what you're needing in the relationship so that you can enter the world of the other person, if only for a brief time. We can't stay in the empathic position permanently, because we could lose ourselves. But empathy is what makes a relationship real — and safe.

Jesus taught about empathy, but in a surprising way: "In everything, do to others what you would have them do to you, for this sums up the Law and the Prophets" (Matt. 7:12). This is a startling teaching, because he didn't condemn our needs as selfish. Instead, he used them as a starting point for learning how to love. In other words, he was saying, "You know how terrible you feel sometimes? That's also how others feel. You know how being loved and understood by another person helps you deal with those feelings? That's also what helps others. Give them what you're also needing."

If we're all taking our needs to safe people, and those safe people are taking their needs to us, love is created—and the Law and the Prophets are fulfilled.

Safe people act on their empathy.

Empathy leads to action. When you see the pain of another, you want to help. God created you that way. We spend time listening to a friend's struggle not because that will make her like us, but because she needs to be understood. We help someone with a problem not so that we'll feel better, but because she is in trouble.

If you want to know how safe someone is, ask yourself: *Is this person with me for him—or for us?* It's no sin to bring your needs to the connection. But it *is* a sin to exploit the relationship for your own ends only.

Look for these warning signs:

When he helps me, he uses it later to get something from me.
I never hear from her unless she's in trouble.
I feel like a mirror, as if my job is to listen and approve.
I'm constantly on the giving end (financially, time, resources).
When my needs come up, he treats them superficially and then
      comes back to himself.

When there's trouble, it will generally show in one person being the chronic "giver" and the other being the chronic "taker."

Love seeks the good of the other: it is "not self-seeking" (1 Cor. 13:5). When you evaluate your relationships, look for people who show genuine concern for your welfare, then make that concern known in concrete actions.

3. Unsafe people resist freedom instead of encouraging it.

We can easily cut to the chase on this interpersonal trait. Ask yourself, *What does the person do with my "no"?*

I was in a support group that met regularly for emotional and spiritual connections. We would all work hard on issues, then reconvene the next week. However, since there was a great deal of authentic caring among the members, those who could would at times get together for dinner or coffee afterward, and "decompress." Over time, the members had grown to enjoy being with each other. "I guess this bonding stuff really works," one member said to me.

One night, however, Josie, a married mother, said, "Rain check for me—I've got to help my kids with homework. See you guys next week."

Brian, another member of the group, said, "Be that way then." His comment was halfway funny, and a couple of people laughed.

Josie didn't laugh. She was hurt, but she didn't say anything until the next meeting. When we met, she told Brian, "I know you were probably joking, but it stung. I spent all week thinking that if I can't go for coffee, then I can't be in the group. I felt like I did when my mother would withdraw if I didn't agree."

Brian felt really bad about hurting Josie and assured her he had been joking. Then he said, "But there's probably some truth to it. I do tend to feel abandoned when someone can't be with me, and I don't like the sadness. So I make sarcastic digs instead."

Brian owned up to his own "unsafe" actions—thus becoming safer. He had a hard time hearing no from others. People would sense his resistance, and they would then distance themselves from him. Brian is becoming safer and safer. But it's those who don't see this in themselves who can be quite destructive. In their eyes, you become bad for being separate from them.

Love protects the separateness of the other. When we are in relationship, the "we" is still "you and me." A safe connection involves two people trusting, opening up, and being honest with each other. Yet the second great theme of relationship, after connection, is separateness.

Separateness is the ability to maintain spiritual and emotional property lines, called boundaries, between you and others. Separate people take responsibility for what is theirs—and they don't take ownership for what isn't theirs.

When we are separate, we bring good things close to our soul, and keep bad things away from us. God created us to stand against what is not from him: "No one who practices deceit will dwell in my house; no one who speaks falsely will stand in my presence" (Ps. 101:7).[1]

Love withers and dies without separateness. It's simply impossible to connect if you are not free to disagree. That kind of love is compliance and people-pleasing. It is not real love. "Am I now trying to win the approval of men, or of God?" asks Paul. "Or am I trying to please men? If I were still trying to please men, I would not be a servant of Christ" (Gal. 1:10).

The opposite of separateness is enmeshment. Enmeshing relationships are those in which one person is swallowed up in the needs of another. In enmeshment, one person feels threatened by the individuality of the other, and actively seeks to control the other by intimidating or manipulating him. In an enmeshing relationship, "together" is bliss (for one), and "apart" is hell (for one). Enmeshment emphasizes similarities and discourages differences in people.

Safe people encourage, value, and nurture the separateness of other people. They understand that they need their own free choices—and that they need to protect the freedom of other people, too. You will always find that the best connections embrace the individual concerns of the other person.

Here are some things to look for in determining safety in this area:

Do they respect my "no" when I state it?
Do they withdraw emotionally when I say no?
Do they get hurt and "make" me feel guilty when I say no?
Do they have a life (interests, hobbies, friends) separate from me?
Do they encourage me to have a separate life too?

Now, you may have never said no in your relationships! This problem may be more your issue than your friend's. So test the waters. Disagree. Be honest. Tell the truth. Choose a value, event, or

---

[1]For more information on separateness, see our book *Boundaries* (Grand Rapids: Zondervan, 1992).

emotion distinct from his. And see what happens. You'll learn a lot about the level of safety in your relationship.

4. Unsafe people flatter us instead of confronting us.

This relational trait is a little more difficult to spot than the previous one. That's because an unsafe person can make you feel very, very good. And a safe person can make you feel very, very bad. It can get confusing. How can you tell the difference?

For several years, I waited tables at various restaurants to pay for graduate school. It was enjoyable work. The money was good. And I liked the people I worked with.

Successful waiters and waitresses come in two flavors: personality and function. The personality types are charming, attentive, and make you feel like your twenty-dollar dinner is an evening at Casablanca. The function types get food there on time and don't bother you. The atmosphere is your own responsibility.

Crystal was, without a doubt, the finest personality waitress I have ever met. All the customers adored her, and the staff as well. She would compliment us on anything and everything: "How is school going? You're in such a fascinating field. Where did you get that gorgeous shirt?" If you came into our restaurant, you would want Crystal to be your waitress.

But one night before work, another waiter came alongside me and said, "Why did you hurt Crystal? The whole staff is upset with you."

I was baffled. "What did I do?" I asked.

"You forgot to take care of a table for her, and she got in trouble with the boss," he said, glaring.

He was right. I remembered I had forgotten the customer, but it had happened several nights ago. I'd seen Crystal many times since then, but she'd said nothing.

I went to her and apologized, saying, "Why didn't you say anything to me?"

She replied, "I didn't want to hurt your feelings."

I tried to put it together. Crystal liked stroking me and avoided confronting me, because that would hurt. Yet she told the staff, and that hurt me more. Crystal could be positive, but she couldn't be directly negative.

Safe relationships are not just about trust, support, and sharing. They are also about truth, righteousness, and honesty. God uses people not only to nurture us, but also to open our eyes to sins, self-ishness, and denial in us. Love also means saying, "I hold this against you," as Jesus did when he confronted the churches (Rev. 2:4, 14, 20).

Being confronted on character issues isn't pleasant. It hurts our self-image. It humbles us. But it doesn't harm us. Loving confronta-tions protect us from our blindness and self-destructiveness. Just as a mother rushes out into a busy street and grabs her child out of traffic, the loving confrontation stops us from walking into disaster.

There is a major difference between confronters and strokers. Confronters (safe ones, not critical-parent types) risk our leaving them to tell us a needed truth. They jeopardize comfort to give us honest love. Strokers, in contrast, lull us to sleep by idealizing our specialness. As long as you feel good, they're happy. This is more addictive than loving. And it certainly isn't safe.

This isn't a diatribe against praise. We all need it: "Let another praise you, and not your own mouth; someone else, and not your own lips" (Prov. 27:2). But praise affirms the truth. Strokers, how-ever, avoid the truth by exclusively praising.

Beware of people who only tell you your good points, justifying it by a desire to be "positive." They aren't loving you enough to tell you when your attitude or behavior is driving your life over a cliff, even though you desperately need to know it.

5. Unsafe people condemn us instead of forgiving us.

Several weeks ago, I (John) forgot to bring my son Ricky, who's five, a toy I'd promised him. He was hurt, and I asked him to forgive me. He said, "What does forgive mean?"

I said, "It means you're not mad anymore so we can be friends."

He thought for a second and said, "Okay, I forgive you."

A few nights later we were having family prayer. When Ricky's turn came, he said, "God, it was way too hot outside today, and I'm kind of frustrated. But I forgive you."

Ricky is learning the nature of forgiveness. When people care about each other, forgiveness restores and reconciles. Forgiveness is the glue of love, making it possible for love to do what it does best: to "bear all things, believe all things, hope all things, endure all things" (1 Cor. 13:7 NASB). These tasks are absolutely impossible without forgiveness. We're just too hard to live with otherwise.

The Bible talks about forgiveness as a legal term. It means to "cancel a debt." This is the central idea behind Jesus' death for us: He paid the penalty for our sins so that we would not have to.

Safe relationships are centered and grounded in forgiveness. When you have a friend with the ability to forgive you for hurting her or letting her down, something deeply spiritual occurs in the transaction between you two. You actually experience a glimpse of the deepest nature of God himself.

People who forgive can—and should—also be people who confront. What is not confessed can't be forgiven. God himself confronts our sins and shows us how we wound him: "I have been hurt by their adulterous hearts which turned away from me, and by their eyes, which played the harlot after their idols" (Ezek. 6:9 NASB). When we are made aware of how we hurt a loved one, then we can be reconciled.

Therefore, you shouldn't discount someone who "has something against you," labeling him as unsafe. He might actually be attempting to come closer in love, in the way that the Bible tells us we are to do.

When we are forgiven by a safe person, several things happen:

He knows our failings.
He neither minimizes nor excuses our sin.
His love for us is greater than our transgression.
He marks "paid in full" and lets it go.
He stays close to us and doesn't abandon us.

That's why the forgiving person is safe. He sees our wrong, yet loves us beyond it. And that love helps heal and transform us into the person God intended. Receiving forgiveness when we know we've truly blown it is a humbling and growth-producing experience. It's the only thing better than forgiving someone else.

On the other hand, an unsafe person who is unable to forgive can be very destructive. Instead of forgiving, she condemns:

She centers on my failings.

She won't let go of the past, even when I've confessed, repented, and made restitution.

She uses my weaknesses to avoid looking at hers.

She sees me as morally inferior to her.

She desires justice more than intimacy.

Unsafe people are often good at identifying your weaknesses. They can quote the minute and hour you hurt them, and recall the scene in intimate detail and living color. Like a good attorney, they have the entire case mapped out. And you are judged "guilty."

Yes, we need to be confronted with our weaknesses. Unsafe people, however, confront us not to forgive us, but to condemn and punish us. They remove their love until we are appropriately chastened. This, obviously, destroys any chance for connection or safety.

6. Unsafe people stay in parent/child roles instead of relating as equals.

Old Mr. Peters, the father of one of my best childhood buddies, had a saying he'd often repeat to us: "I agree with what you're saying, but I don't agree with your right to say it."

Now, you had to be listening to that one to catch it. It sounded so much like the old "agreeing to disagree" line. And, when he'd see us cock our heads quizzically like confused puppies, he'd laugh, knowing he'd gotten us.

Mr. Peters' play on words, however, describes the next issue very well. Safe people respect our right to make decisions and adult choices. Unsafe people resist our adult functioning. They "don't agree with our right" to an opinion, a value, or a decision. Unsafe people react to our adultness by withdrawing from it.

This is the opposite of how safe people relate to us. Safe individuals love to see us grow up and mature, and they rejoice when we carry out our responsibility to "fill the earth and subdue it" (Gen. 1:28). They want to see us develop our God-given gifts and talents and use them. Safe people love to see adults being formed.

This is true in all relationships, and especially in parenting. When the Bible tells us to "Train a child in the way he should go, and when he is old he will not turn from it" (Prov. 22:6), this doesn't mean you should decide where the child is to go. Instead, you should help the child discover God's path for her—even if that means a path you might not have chosen.

The same is true in our friendships. Your closest relationships are, at all times, actively working either for or against your growth. In the list below, the first two ways of relating hinder your growth, and the last one encourages it:

I feel like a kid around them.
I feel like I have to be their parent.
I feel equal with them.

I feel like a kid around them.

In this first type of relationship, you often feel controlled or criticized. The parental person acts as if you can't make decisions for yourself regarding values, money, job, theology, sex, or politics. He feels resentful when you attempt any major decisions without his approval. So he withholds approval of your decisions until you again resign yourself to being his child—even if you're in your middle-age years.

Authority roles often lend themselves to these kinds of dynamics. For example, bosses, teachers, doctors, and police often act parental, as in "the boss put me down again and made me feel like a child." It's important to separate roles from character here. While some parental-types do seek out roles where they can push people around, some just want to do a good job.

Here are things to look for in the parental person:

He gives me advice without asking if I want it.
He doesn't trust my judgment.
He thinks I need his help in navigating through life.
He is critical.
He is disapproving.
He withdraws when I make adult decisions with which he disagrees.

Now, suppose you are exquisitely sensitive to critical people. When they confront you, you immediately question your decisions. Put this character problem with a parental-type person—and you have major problems.

I feel like I have to be their parent.

You can also have the opposite type of relationship. Here, the roles are reversed. You're trying to relate to a person who wants you to be the parent. Here's a hint that there's a problem: They are neither under eighteen years old nor under your legal guardianship.

With this second subtype of unsafety, your friend is afraid of adulthood with its responsibilities and risks. Can't fault him for that. But the problem emerges in what he sees as your role: you become either the approval-providing parent, or the authoritarian controller in his head.

For example, he may pressure you to tell him what to do: what clothes to buy, where to work, and what women to date. He may ask you to interpret the Bible for him. On the other hand, he may act like a rebellious adolescent around you, constantly challenging you and accusing you of being controlling.

Neither of these child positions are mature. Both are unsafe. One is overcompliant, and one is overreactive. And they can hurt you by not allowing you simply to be an adult: You be you and I'll be me, and we'll respect each other. There's always a power struggle going on here.

I feel equal with them.

The safe person doesn't make you become either a child or a parent. He takes ownership of his life, talents, and values. He wants to "seek first [God's] kingdom and his righteousness" (Matt. 6:33) on his own, but with your consultation—not your approval. And he wants you to flourish in your life—without needing his approval. Even if you disagree.

You know you're around a safe, adult person by the following characteristics:

She is not threatened by your differences.

She has standards, values, and convictions she's worked out for herself.

At the same time, she doesn't have a "right way" and a "wrong way" for everything.

She functions at least on the same level of maturity as her same-age peers.

She appreciates mystery and the unknown.
She encourages me to develop my own values.

Remember that we want our efforts to be approved by God (2 Tim. 2:15), not people. Find people who want the same goal for you.

7. Unsafe people are unstable over time instead of being consistent.

Are you the romantic/trusting/naive type? If so, you're particularly vulnerable to unsafe people because you tend to trust people immediately instead of putting them through the test of time. As clichéd as it may sound, time is indeed the best judge of character.

Who we are and what we do are very, very related. Character can't be completely hidden over a lifetime; it leaks out sooner or later. As Jesus said, "What you have said in the dark will be heard in the daylight, and what you have whispered in the ear in the inner rooms will be proclaimed from the housetops" (Luke 12:3). So hiding and pretending aren't ever going to pay off for us.

And time tends to prove out the truth. As time passes, spouses, for example, learn the truth about each other's ability to love, to listen, to be responsible, and to forgive. No matter what one says, the other one has years of memories that will either confirm or deny that person's words.

Bernard is a friend of mine who constantly writes emotional checks he can't cash. Bernard is caring, helpful, and enjoyable to be with. Everybody loves him. And he really loves people. But Bernard is a relational sprinter, not a marathoner. He's there for you if you're there. But it's hard for Bernard to keep you in mind when he's off helping another person.

This trait has caused Bernard to be unsafe with his friends and family. They have learned the hard way that you cannot depend on him. He commits and commits and commits—but he does not come through. If you ask him to return the lawnmower he borrowed last week, don't block out your mowing hours on your schedule anytime soon.

Bernard isn't a bad person, nor is he insincere. But he loves the intense warmth of being close to a person in the here-and-now. It gets somewhat addictive to him, and he can't delay gratification to help a person who isn't around, when another, in-the-flesh person is available. And so he routinely disappoints himself and his friends. He flunks the time test.

For example, when Bernard and I would plan dinners or nights out, he was often late, and sometimes he wouldn't show up at all. Of course he'd always have a great excuse about some emergency or crisis. Finally, I realized I wasn't a "crisis," so I didn't make the cut. I learned that, over time, I shouldn't depend on Bernard.

Safety isn't like that. People who pass the test of time are "timeless" people. They guard your trust as if it were money in the bank. They are stable and reliable in their emotional commitments.

That's why time-friendly people tend to make fewer emotional commitments than my friend Bernard does. They have a profound understanding of how much time it takes to be there for someone, so they think, deliberate, and pray long and hard before they decide to invest in a relationship. You might think they're aloof or uncaring. They're not. They are, instead, unwilling to write bad checks, emotionally speaking.

Another friend, Pamela, recently passed the time test with flying colors. We've known each other a long time, and I needed her input on a big decision I was making. I knew she was busy, but I called her anyway, asking, "Can we do lunch?"

Pamela lives quite a drive away, but she checked her calendar (another trait of safe people!), and we made an appointment. A few days later, we met, and I told her how much it meant to me for her to take the time out for me.

She was genuinely surprised. "Well, I told you I'd be here, didn't I?" Tears came to my eyes. For Pamela, a relationship means that you're there for good. End of conversation.

Look for people who are "anchored" over time. Don't go for flashy, intense, addictive types. A Ford that will be there tomorrow is a lot better than a Maserati that might be gone. There are stable Maseratis. But it's best to drive them awhile, that is, test out the relationship over time, to make sure.

Here are some traits to look for in your relationships:

Are they living up to their commitments to me?
Are they here for me only when I'm here?
Do they tell me no when they don't have time?
Do they make promises they can't keep?

Am I the last in a string of broken relationships?

Do others warn me about their pattern of relating?

Love is abiding, timeless, and unchanging, just like its Author. Find people who love you, and love you well over time, like he does: "Jesus Christ is the same yesterday and today and forever" (Heb. 13:8).

8. **Unsafe people are a negative influence on us, rather than a positive one.**

In my first decade as a Christian, I (John) hung around all sorts of groups, theological persuasions, and personality types. I suppose I was searching for the kind of believers with whom I fit, and who seemed to fit me. Part of that journey involved a guy named Harry.

I respected Harry. He seemed to have his spiritual act together. He was one of those people who'd been spending at least an hour a day in devotions for years. He witnessed regularly and taught a Bible study. He had strong convictions, and he'd done it the hard way: by searching the Bible, not by piggybacking on someone else.

I respected Harry, but I didn't always feel safe around him. I found that as long as my life was together, we got along. But if my weaknesses leaked out, I'd have to endure a lecture, or, what was worse, a feeling of disapproval. So I hid my flaws and remained "victorious."

The problem was, in small ways, I started becoming a "Harry junior." I presented my strong side to the world and stayed away from failure. And I adopted Harry's theology, which was to evaluate all your actions by their value to the kingdom of God. If your action helped people spiritually, it was good. If not, it was at best a waste of time, and at worst it was out-and-out destructive. Harry's warped approach to spirituality did not take into account the actual components of good relationships: love, belonging, trust, togetherness, and so forth. These qualities, however, are also of great value to the kingdom of God (Matt. 22:37–40).

I saw this vividly when I visited my parents' home, where two of my three sisters, Susan and Cris, were still living. They ran up to me excitedly when I walked in the front door. "Can you play Monopoly with us?" they asked.

Now, Monopoly was a favorite family addiction. We'd spent many rainy days bankrupting each other. But now things were different. I was a *spiritual* man. I had *priorities*.

So I said what I thought any spiritual man would say: "No thanks. Monopoly doesn't change your life."

My sisters were crushed. They didn't say anything at the time, but I learned later that they felt like I'd changed. And not for the better.

Yet Harry would have approved of my refusal to play with my sisters. I'd seen him say the same things several times to friends who wanted to play tennis or see a movie. At the time, I thought he was being spiritual. Now I know that his criticisms covered up his inability to make deep relationships.

Instead of making me more "spiritual," Harry brought out the worst in me. I became aloof, critical, and judgmental. Harry was an unsafe person because, while I was around him, my other relationships suffered.

Safety breeds safety. And safe people make us better people for being around them. This is Jesus' "fruit test": "No good tree bears bad fruit, nor does a bad tree bear good fruit" (Luke 6:43). We cannot fail to be influenced, for better or worse, by the people in whom we invest. It will always show: "Bad company corrupts good character" (1 Cor. 15:33). And good company builds up our hearts.

An unsafe person may make you feel good—yet wound you emotionally. She may make you act better, but hurt your character. And you may think you're being treated well, but she may be hindering your growth. Fruit is about character issues—not symptoms.

The woman who is swept off her feet by an insincere charmer is a good example of this. She feels wonderful: loved, pursued, intoxicated by the attentiveness and flattery of the charmer. Her infatuation may make her more caring for her friends, more patient and forgiving. Her cup feels so full that she can give more.

But the reality is that while she feels and acts better, she is in the middle of a fantasy that will someday come crashing down around her. She is not being prepared for a real relationship, in which you deal with the imperfections of yourself and the other person. So she falls very hard, and sometimes she can't trust again for a long time.

Safe people are not perfect, but they help us progress toward Christlike character in the four major areas of spiritual growth. Ask yourself these questions about the people with whom you relate. As a result of spending time with this person, am I

more loving or more detached?
more honest or more compliant?
more forgiving or more idealistic?
more mutual or more childish?

Deciding whether a relationship is good for you will take time and some long, hard, coldly objective analysis. And it will probably take a friend's detached eye. But look at your relationships over the long haul, and judge them for how they have changed your life—for better or worse.

9. Unsafe people gossip instead of keeping secrets.

We all have experiences, thoughts, emotions, or behaviors that we don't feel safe telling the world. We need someone in whom to confide. Some of us have secret sins that plague us. Others have been victimized or abused. Still others simply need a person to tell our private stories to.

Few things are more bruising than having our secrets betrayed. If you have ever entrusted part of yourself to another, and then heard about it from a third party, you have been triangulated. Triangulation occurs when person A tells a secret to person B, who then tells person C about it. Triangulation is a form of what the Bible calls "gossip": "A gossip betrays a confidence, but a trustworthy man keeps a secret" (Prov. 11:13).

Often, a triangulator will try to justify his untrustworthiness by different excuses, such as:

It just slipped out.
It wasn't that serious. You're overreacting.
It was for your own good.
They made me tell.

But just as often the truth has more to do with the unsafe person. He may be unable to confront people directly, so he does it behind their backs. He may feel insignificant, so gossip gives him the sense that he is important and on the "inside track." He may be pitting one person against another in a repetitive pattern from childhood. Or he may simply lack a sense of empathy for the terrible pain that gossip brings to others.

No matter what, this is nothing but destructive. We all need a place for our secrets to be held and respected. Secrets don't get well without relationship. We're all looking for safe relationships where someone knows all of our parts. So, when you divulge a private matter with another, it's a big deal. You are taking a risk with an important part of your soul. And when confidence is broken, so is trust, hope, and healing.

Not only this, but also relationships can be torn apart between friends. Persons A and C can be alienated by the triangulator. This is what people mean when they say, "She came between us." A triangulator has been at work.

A safe person will hold confidences. He will not use your secrets for his own needs. "A perverse man stirs up dissension, and a gossip separates close friends" (Prov. 16:28).

The eighteeth-century English preacher George Whitefield is a good example of a safe person. With John Wesley, Whitefield was one of the founders of the Methodist Church. Yet he disagreed heartily with Wesley's theology, and the two men were well known for their differences.

One day, a reporter asked Whitefield, "Reverend, do you think you will see John Wesley in heaven?" This question was an invitation to triangulation between two opponents.

"No, I do not," replied Whitefield.

"Why is that?" asked the surprised reporter.

Whitefield answered, "Because I believe that John Wesley will be so close to the bosom of God that we will not be able to see him for the surrounding glory." George Whitefield would not attack a person who was not there to defend himself. Look for people who can hold your secrets.

Conclusion

Now that we've finished with our section on understanding who's safe and who isn't, here's a very important point: Don't stop reading the book.

The reason is simple. Odds are, even with this road map of character to evaluate your relationships, you will still choose unsafe people. You will still find the same painful lapses in judgment. You will still suffer in the same ways.

That's because the problem is often inside us. We have needs, conflicts, and misperceptions that drive us toward unsafe people. And, until we address them, we'll continue seeking unsafe people "as a dog returns to its vomit" (Prov. 26:11).

To best deal with unsafe people, we first need to understand what causes us to be unsafe. For the problem is not just *outside* us; it is *inside* every one of us. As we'll see in the next chapter, unsafety finds its origin in sin. And sin—as we know—is everyone's problem (Rom. 3:23).

CHAPTER FOUR

How We Lost Our Safety

I REMEMBER THE DAY my son Ricky learned about unsafe people.

It began with a yowl and a crash in the living room. My wife and I hurried in to investigate. What we encountered was a broken lamp, a rapidly disappearing cat, and two preschoolers frozen in position.

We'd been through these scenarios often enough that I figured out what had happened by the evidence: Ricky, who was four, had probably pulled the cat's tail again. Stripey had struggled to get away and had knocked over the lamp in her exit. Benny, two, was an innocent bystander.

Normally, I would ask the boys what happened, but I was tired. I'd had a long day, and I was convinced of Ricky's guilt by his long history of tail-pulling. I ordered a time-out.

"But I didn't do it!" he protested.

I ignored him. After all, lots of guilty kids protest their innocence. But this time Ricky didn't settle down into his jail sentence. He began sobbing.

Then the unexpected happened. Benny walked up to me and said, "Dad, I did it."

At that awful moment I questioned my calling and competence as a father. I had wrongly accused and disciplined Ricky without listening to his side of things. So, with great remorse for his pain, I apologized to my son and asked his forgiveness.

Thankfully, kids seem to recover quickly from these sorts of injuries if the parents acknowledge their mistake. Within a few minutes, Ricky and I were wrestling on the floor.

But one thing stands out about this incident: the look on my son's face. When he realized that no matter what he said, he was going to the time-out corner, I remembered seeing a curious expression on his face. It wasn't sadness or anger, which came within a few seconds. But first, it was *surprise*.

Surprise. Disbelief. For a brief time, Ricky experienced a shift in his understanding of the world. He'd thought parents were fair. He'd thought that if you were innocent, bad things didn't happen to you. He'd thought that Dad would believe he was telling the truth.

And now, it was as if the rules of life no longer applied, as if gravity were suspended. Dad wasn't as safe as he'd thought. Ricky lost a little of his innocence that day. He began learning about the effects of the Fall.

The Sad Truth

Many of us can relate to Ricky's experience. The first time we get hurt by an unsafe person—or even a reasonably safe one—there is always a period of surprise as we begin the painful adjustment to the realities of unsafety. We begin grieving our wishes for a perfectly safe, dependable world.

This is not an easy step. It's hard knowing we live in a universe in which we're vulnerable to unsafe individuals. People matter to us, and they can deeply injure us.

A father, wanting to teach his six-year-old daughter about the world, had her stand on the edge of her bed. He stood a couple of feet away, and said, "Jump, honey, I'll catch you."

Hesitantly, the little girl gathered herself and leaped off the bed. Her father moved back and let her fall to the floor. When she hit, she cried, "Why did you drop me, Dad?"

"Because," said the father, "I want you to learn not to trust anyone."

The girl's father made a grave error in teaching the realities of the world. We have to experience trustworthy love before we can deal with an untrustworthy world. If we have no place to learn about dependable, safe people, we will never be able to sustain ourselves. The father would have done better to let her see his inevitable imperfections emerge, then teach her about not expecting perfection.

If, like Ricky and the girl in the story, you've been surprised by unsafety, it's often helpful to understand how we lost our safety. But first we need to look at the world that God intended for us to have.

God Created a Safe World

God never intended for us to suffer the effects of an unsafe world. Instead, he created a safe world, where Adam and Eve lived in harmony with him, each other, and themselves.

One of Jesus' deepest concerns was our people-to-people connection. He called this "being one" in his high priestly prayer: "that all of them may be one, Father, just as you are in me and I am in you. May they also be in us so that the world may believe that you have sent me" (John 17:21). Our safe relationships with others testify to the world about God's safe love for us. He meant us to be "in" each other, just as the Father and the Son are. Imagine that: We are to internalize, or take in, love from one another and use it, just as God does.

And Then Came Sin ...

However, our state of unity and harmonious relationship was not to be. What theologians call the fall from grace changed the nature of relationships forever. Sin entered the world through Satan, Adam, and Eve, and it manifested itself in four areas: sin by us, sin against us, sin in the world, and Satan's strategies.

Sin by Us

Ever had a car mechanic or a doctor ask you, "Do you want the good news or the bad news first?" I always opt for the latter—then the bad news is out of the way.

When we look at the different ways the Fall hurt our safety, let's look at the bad news first. The bad news is, *some* of this is our fault. The good news is, not *all* of this is our fault.

We all have a sinful nature that we inherited from our first parents, the first dysfunctional family, Adam and Eve. When they gave in to the temptation to deny their humble dependence on the Creator, and "be like God, knowing good and evil" (Gen. 3:5), they damaged their relationship with God and with each other.

Our sinful nature is widely misunderstood. It's common, for example, to think that our sinful inclinations are only a desire to do "bad things." The sinful self also makes me want to hurt others, be lazy, commit adultery, have a bad attitude, and so on.

For example, Randy went to his men's support group hesitantly, head hanging low. Though married to a loving wife, he had struggled with pornography for several years. The day before his group meeting, he had gone to the adult bookstore during lunch. Now, confessing his problem to his friends, Randy said, "Well, guys, it happened again. That old sin nature won out today. Guess I wasn't in the Word enough."

This approach to sin is quite popular because it sounds scriptural. However, this approach is biblically inadequate and incomplete. The truth is, our sinful nature is also our inclination to live without God. In our pride, we come to despise our dependency and powerlessness. We want to be the Creator, not the creature.

Satan, the first to rebel against God, declared: "I will ascend above the tops of the clouds; I will make myself like the Most High" (Isa.14:14). Satan resented his "lowly" position of having to depend on and give authority to God. He couldn't accept his creatureliness.

Satan then turned around and offered the same deal to Adam and Eve. "If you eat from the tree that God forbids you," he said, "you will be like God!" Adam and Eve bit on the offer, and the rest is history. From Adam and Eve we were infected with the disease and the desire to live without God.

Sin also set into play four more dynamics that are seriously destructive to our safety: (1) we are envious; (2) we think we are self-sufficient; (3) we think we are entitled to special treatment; and (4) we transgress against God's laws. Let's look at each of these four areas.

1. We are envious.

Paula was a single mother who had reentered the dating world. It wasn't a lot of fun out there, but she did want to date and marry a Christian guy. Her friend Margie had never married and was quite shy about meeting men. To keep each other company in the shark tank called dating life, they often accompanied one another to church functions and socials.

Margie soon noticed Brad, a likable single man, and set her sights on him. But being reserved, she was having a hard time letting Brad know about her interest. Paula, on the other hand, had quickly met another man, Chuck, and within a few weeks they had been out several times.

Over lunch one day, Margie said to Paula, "How come things are going so well for you? You've already had a chance at marriage—I haven't even been up to bat! That's not fair!" Because of her envy, Margie was unable to cheerlead Paula on to more relational success, and as a result their relationship suffered.

That's how envy can spoil safety. Envy makes us resent people who have something we don't have. It feeds on itself and is ultimately self-destructive. When we envy, the very people who are loving, safe, and generous become the bad guys in our eyes.

All of us are tainted with envy. Envy is intimately connected with coveting, and is best defined as a tendency to hate other people for having what we want. Envy says, "What is inside me is bad. What is outside me is good. I hate anyone who has something I desire."

Jesus taught about envy in the parable of the workers. A laborer worked in the hot sun all day for a boss, and accepted a denarius for it, a fair wage in those days. Yet, one hour before the end of the day, his employer hired another man and paid him a denarius for that one hour.

Enraged at what he thought was unfairness, the laborer complained to his boss, who replied: "Friend, I am not being unfair to you. Didn't you agree to work for a denarius? Take your pay and go. I want to give the man who was hired last the same as I gave you. Don't I have the right to do what I want with my own money? Or are you envious because I am generous?" (Matt. 20:13–15).

Envy makes generosity sound unfair. It is the opposite of love, which "does not envy ... but rejoices with the truth" (1 Cor. 13:4, 6). Remember that the chief priests handed Jesus over to Pilate out of envy (Mark 15:10). They hated that he had more love inside him than they did.

Envy is a fundamental result of the sinful nature. In fact, Christian philosopher Francis Schaeffer says that every one of the Ten Commandments can be summed up in the last: "You shall not covet" (Ex. 20:17). He states, "Any time that we break one of the other commandments of God, it means that we have already broken this commandment, in coveting." In other words, coveting causes outward sin.

Envy is very different from need. When we need something from someone else, that person is free to say no to our request. Suppose I ask my friend to go on vacation with me, but he can't because he's busy that week. If I were acting out of need, I would be sad that my friend could not go, but I wouldn't consider him bad for not coming; he's just busy.

That's not how envy operates. If I were acting out of envy, I would resent my friend's freedom to say no. When we envy, we make the other person bad for not giving us what we need. Envy says, "I'm angry that you don't want to go on vacation with me. You must not care about me." Envy wants to control love, and in so doing, it destroys love.

How does envy destroy our safety? By spoiling any chance to be loved. When we envy, we resent those who have something to offer us. And, if they do give us something we need, envy makes us (1) devalue what we just got, because our need is insatiable, and (2) resent the giver, because he or she could have always given more.

Begin to be aware of your tendency to make the "haves" bad and the "have nots" good. Ask God to help you to be grateful for what you have, and to rejoice in the good things that others have. Then you'll be able to take in more of the safe people who may be waiting for you to ask them for help.

2. We think we are self-sufficient.

God has created all of us incomplete, inadequate, and in need of a huge shopping list full of ingredients that we cannot provide ourselves. This list includes things like God's love and provision, the love of other people, and our physical needs. Yet we desire to be a universe unto ourselves. Deep within, all of us hate the idea of having to need others, having to ask for what we don't have, having to bow the knee to God. We resist admitting we can't make it on our own, that we don't have it together. We do not want to admit our impoverishment, because it's humiliating.

Satan said he would raise his throne "above the stars of God" (Isa. 14:13). He hated being dependent on God. Men built the tower

of Babel to be self-sufficient: "that we may make a name for ourselves and not be scattered over the face of the whole earth" (Gen.
11:4). The Laodicean church pretended they had no needs and were
confronted for it: "You say, 'I am rich; I have acquired wealth and do
not need a thing.' But you do not realize that you are wretched, piti-
ful, poor, blind and naked" (Rev. 3:17).

The problem is, we often teach self-sufficiency as a positive
character trait. It's common for hurting Christians who reach out
with depression, anxiety, marriage problems, and family issues to be
told, "You don't have enough faith" or "You aren't victorious
enough." We think that the individual who doesn't have problems
(or who hides his problems) is the model for maturity. This is a far
cry from what Jesus taught in his parable of the Pharisee and the tax
collector. The screwed-up, needy tax man cried out about all his sin
and neediness to God, and "went home justified" (Luke 18:14). The
Pharisee, however, went home empty-handed.

How does our self-sufficiency ruin safety? Primarily by prevent-
ing us from experiencing our impoverishment. People who "have it
together" are not hungry, or thirsty, for others. They do not feel a
lack within when they're alone or in distress. They do not connect
with other people, because they do not experience any need for it.

Adults who grow up in military families often report this
dynamic. They'll move twelve times in as many years, and they
quickly realize that they probably won't see their classmates ever
again after each school year. To survive, they simply construct an
adaptive front that lets them make a few acquaintances and not get
rejected by the class, and that's it. No one gets inside, no one gets
close. They stay self-sufficient to keep from experiencing overwhelming loss and abandonment. And they often hold it together
until they grow up and try to pull off a marriage—at which time disaster erupts.

Make friends with your needs. Welcome them. They are a gift
from God, designed to draw you into relationship with him and with
his safe people. Your needs are the cure to the sin of self-sufficiency.

3. We think we are entitled to special treatment.

The sin nature also causes a sense of entitlement. Not only did
Satan envy God's goodness, not only did he wish to be self-sufficient,

but he also felt he deserved privileged treatment: "I will ascend
above the tops of the clouds" (Isa.14:14). In other words, "Godhood
is my right and my prerogative."

Just as envy is different from need, so is a sense of entitlement.
Need says, "I'm hungry and thirsty. Please give me something to eat
and drink." Entitlement says, "By virtue of who I am, you must give
me something to eat and drink." People who feel they are entitled
to something are self-absorbed and grandiose.

Jonah is a book about entitlement. The Israelite prophet
enjoyed the special status of being one of the chosen people of God.
So when God was merciful to Nineveh's people, Jonah became
enraged at God. He prayed, "O LORD, is this not what I said when I
was still at home? That is why I was so quick to flee to Tarshish. I
knew that you are a gracious and compassionate God, slow to anger
and abounding in love, a God who relents from sending calamity.
Now, O LORD, take away my life, for it is better for me to die than to
live" (Jonah 4:2–3).

Instead of rejoicing at the grace of God, Jonah had a tantrum. In
his mind, he and his people had lost their privileged position,
because there was enough of God for Israel and Nineveh both.

Entitlement is a demand for special treatment. Instead of being
grateful for ordinary, "good-enough" resources and situations, we
demand the best. Here are a few examples of entitlement:

feeling that I deserve a better lot in life than I received
a sense that people need to make restitution for their sins
    against me
a need for others to apologize for hurting me before I will get
    better
an inability to feel loved when I am not front and center stage
a sense of deprivation when I am not made special to others
feeling that people don't treat me with the respect I deserve

Obviously, entitlement destroys safety, because no normal
human can fulfill our demands! It's impossible to love an entitled
person, as some fault, empathic misstep, or insensitivity will send
the entire relationship tumbling down. The entitled person must be
listened to and understood perfectly at all times, or she feels injured
and wounded. The end result is isolation.

The antidote to entitlement is forgiveness in two directions. We need to ask forgiveness for our own imperfections. And we need to learn to forgive others for not meeting our outrageous expectations.

4. We transgress against God's laws.

Finally, the sin nature emerges in an attitude of transgression. When we transgress, we violate a boundary that God has set down. This is the aspect of our sinful nature that rebels against having any restrictions. For example, Adam and Eve had lots of yeses from God, lots of freedom. They only had one no: Don't eat from the tree of the knowledge of good and evil. And they crossed the only limit he had set.

This tendency to break the rules of God is deliberate. It chooses indulging self over loving God: "Keep your servant also from willful sins; may they not rule over me. Then will I be blameless, innocent of great transgression" (Ps. 19:13).

When we refuse to be kind to someone when it would be right to do it; when we lie to each other; when we lash out in violence, we transgress, disregarding the standards and statutes of God. And with our transgressions, we destroy the safety in our relationships.

Sometimes we transgress because we like to rebel. For example, a teenager may drink because he likes to break the rules. Sometimes we transgress because of emotional problems. For example, a divorced single mother may drink because she is trying to anesthetize the pain of her disconnectedness. Both teenager and mother are responsible for their destructive actions and attitudes. But we first need to understand why each person is transgressing in order to help him or her.

Envy, self-sufficiency, entitlement, and transgressions push us further into isolation. The result of that isolation is generally some sort of breakdown. Like a car running out of gas, we stop functioning well. We act out our addictions, get depressed, and function poorly in our relationships. However, these "bad deeds" are only a symptom of the deeper problem: the disconnection caused by envy, self-sufficiency, entitlement, and transgressions.

Too often, we chalk up a behavioral problem to "sin" and decide to pray more, when more likely than not, it's the isolation that caused the problem, and the "big four" which caused the isolation. To put it even more clearly:

Our sinful nature breeds envy, self-sufficiency, entitlement, and transgression.

Envy, self-sufficiency, entitlement, and transgression breed isolation.

Isolation breeds life problems (emotional, behavioral, relational).

For example, remember Randy, whom we met at the beginning of the chapter? He sinned sexually and confessed to his support group that his problem was that he wasn't in the Word enough. That may have been a big part of it, for connection with God is essential.

Randy, however, didn't mention that he'd had some major losses recently, with job demotions, problems with his children, and an extremely painful rift with his wife. And, as he later found out, he had a clear pattern. When he would encounter losses or overwhelming stress, he would go to pornography for support instead of his friends. They would only find out about his problem later, during his confessions.

As Randy became more aware his pattern of going to pornography for comfort, he took the steps of calling friends when he felt alone and anxious—*before* he sinned behaviorally. And gradually he felt less and less need to act out. As he acknowledged his need for connection with God and other people, his sinful behavior diminished.

Sin Against Us

Congratulations! You made it through the bad news! Not that this next section is less important, but it's always better to look at our own fault first. As Jesus told us, "First take the plank out of your own eye, and then you will see clearly to remove the speck from your brother's eye" (Matt. 7:5).

The Fall produced a second reason we lose safety: sin against us. Not only are we perpetrators of evil, but we are also victims of it. We are sinful, but we are also sinned against.

The Bible presents many illustrations of this principle. For example, God calls this "punishing the children for the sin of the fathers to the third and fourth generation of those who hate me" (Ex. 20:5). Anyone who has come from an alcoholic family background can attest to this. In a fallen world, the innocent suffer for the evil of others.

Why do the innocent suffer? Because of love. God designed love to be based on our free will. He didn't want to be loved out of fear, or out of compliance. He wanted to be loved out of gratitude. But love has a price tag. If love is free, then a lover is free to be unloving. Otherwise love is forced. Because we are free to be unloving, many of us have been run over by the steamroller of the selfishness of others.

How do sins against us destroy safety? Basically, by destroying our ability to connect with others in helpful ways. This breakdown occurs all through life, but begins in childhood, during our developmental years.

Let's look at four ways that sins against us may have affected our development: (1) our bonding process was disrupted; (2) our boundaries were not respected; (3) we were not seen as whole people, with good and bad traits; and (4) we were not allowed to mature into adults. Any of these sins against us may affect our ability to form relationships with safe people.[1]

1. Our bonding process was disrupted.

Our first and deepest need as human beings is to bond, to attach to another, to trust another, to belong. Just as a baby needs her mother and panics when she isn't present, we need each other's presence. Bonded people are able to reach out for comfort and receive it.

However, the bonding process is often disrupted in the following ways:

Detachment: someone being emotionally inaccessible to us
Abandonment: someone connecting, then leaving
Inconsistency: someone being unstable as a love object
Criticism: unloving attacks upon our needy aspects
Abuse: violations of our soul that destroy trust

---

[1]For a full treatment on the four needs, refer to *Changes That Heal* by Dr. Henry Cloud (Grand Rapids: Zondervan, 1992) and *Hiding from Love* by Dr. John Townsend (Colorado Springs: NavPress, 1991).

These problems can be devastating to the long process of learning to trust God and people. The person who experiences disruption of bonding recoils and withdraws emotionally. He does not experience his need, the hunger for love. Instead, he buries his needs deep inside, so he can no longer be hurt.

This withdrawal is called *defensive devaluation*. Defensive devaluation is a protective device that makes love bad, trust unimportant, and people "no darn good" anyway. People who have been deeply hurt in their relationships will often devalue love so it doesn't hurt so much. And they often become resigned to never loving again.

People who are unbonded do funny things in relationships:

They don't look for safe people: there's no hunger.
They don't recognize safe people: no one is safe.
They don't reach out to safe people: why get hurt again?

Although unbonded people often have friends and families, their isolation is deep and can cause many serious problems.

A person who cannot bond may suffer from addictions, depression, emptiness, excessive caretaking, fear of being treated like an object, fears of closeness, feelings of guilt, feelings of unreality, idealism, lack of joy, loss of meaning, negative bonds, outbursts of anger, panic, shallow relationships, or thought problems such as confusion, distorted thinking, and irrational fears.

I (John) remember being confronted in a growth group at seminary by my peers. They told me something like, "Thanks for supporting us. But we know nothing of you. And we'd like to." I remember having absolutely nothing to say to these guys. It was as if they had asked me to explain nuclear physics. I stammered something, but it was obvious I had been devaluing what the group could do for me.

Are you unbonded? Has your ability to be vulnerable, to be needy, to trust been disrupted? Do you find yourself devaluing safe people? If so, you may need to find a healing setting like a recovery-based church or a counselor to deal with your bonding injuries.

2. Our boundaries were not respected.

Our second developmental need is to learn boundaries. Boundaries are our spiritual and emotional "property lines." They tell us where we end, and where others begin. They help to keep good things in us, and bad things out. We take responsibility for what is ours, and not for what isn't. When we are clearly defined, we can carry our own loads, and we know when it's appropriate to help others with their burdens (Gal. 6:1–5).[2]

Yet our ability to say no can also be sinned against. We can be hurt in our ability to set limits, establish consequences, and not rescue others. Here are some ways our boundaries can be injured:

Aggressive control: someone hurting us if we say no
Passive control: someone leaving us if we say no
Regressive control: guilt messages if we say no
Limitlessness: someone never saying no to us

These dynamics are common in most relationships, and are extremely destructive to our ability to conduct our lives responsibly. But how do boundary injuries hurt our safety?

Basically, if an unbonded person can't take love in, a boundaryless person can't keep love in. Like a cup with no bottom, the grace and care the boundaryless person receives often cannot stay inside to nourish and sustain them.

First, boundaryless people tend to feel abandoned when there is distance. Because they've often been punished by abandonment, they don't have the ability to stand apart, to be alone, and to hold firm in conflict. So when they're in an argument with a rageaholic who's screaming like a banshee, boundaryless people are cast into a panic state that they must get out of by complying with the wishes of the screamer.

Second, boundaryless people tend to isolate as their only limit. Often, people with weak boundaries will give in repeatedly to some irresponsible or demanding person. Then, out of the blue, they'll pack up and leave the relationship with no warning. This is because they were unable to set and keep limits at early stages when there were problems. They didn't have the resources to, at the right times, "speak the truth in love" (Eph. 4:15).

This also destroys our safety. If your boundaries have been injured, you may find that when you are in conflict with someone, you shut down without even being aware of it. This isolates us from love, and keeps us from taking in safe people.

---

[2]For more information, refer to *Boundaries* (Grand Rapids, Zondervan: 1992).

Kate had been quite controlled by her overprotective mother. She'd always been warned that she was sickly, would get hit by cars, and didn't know how to care for herself well. So she fulfilled all those prophecies.

Having no sense of strong boundaries, Kate had great difficulty taking risks and connecting with people. The only safe people were at her home. Finally, however, with a supportive church group, Kate set limits on her time with her mom, made friends in her singles' group, and stayed connected to her new spiritual family.

People who have trouble with boundaries may exhibit the following symptoms: blaming others, codependency, depression, difficulties with being alone, disorganization and lack of direction, extreme dependency, feelings of being let down, feelings of obligation, generalized anxiety, identity confusion, impulsiveness, inability to say no, isolation, masochism, overresponsibility and guilt, panic, passive-aggressive behavior, procrastination and inability to follow through, resentment, substance abuse and eating disorders, thought problems and obsessive-compulsive problems, underresponsibility, and victim mentality.

3. We were not seen as whole people, with good and bad traits.

Our third developmental need is the ability to resolve the split between goodness and badness. After we answer who loves me (bonding) and who am I (boundaries), we need to know, am I good or bad?

We all have a problem in this area. We weren't intended to be bad, but in many ways we are. We all long to be back in the Garden, in a state of unbroken love with God and others. Coming to terms with badness involves great loss and struggle for us.

Paul echoes this anguish in his cry, "For what I want to do I do not do, but what I hate I do" (Rom. 7:15). He understood that, even as Christians, we still sin, struggle, and fail. All the good intentions, commitment, and willpower in the world won't change that reality.

Resolving good-bad issues is something God never had to do in himself. He had no badness to contend with. However, he had to come up with solutions for his fallen human race. That's what makes Christianity unique. We have a perfect God dying for a sinful people. Even more incredible, this sinful people doesn't have to be good to be loved. We can be bad and still be loved, just as the prodigal son was (Luke 15:11–32). But many of us have learned that we are not loved when we are bad.

Injuries in this area occur in four ways:

Perfectionism: others expecting us to have no faults
Idealization: others denying our imperfections
Shaming: others condemning our negative qualities
Splitting: others seeing us as all-good or all-bad

These relational patterns in significant relationships can create a dedicated perfectionist, fully committed to the concept that she can and must eradicate any negative traits—and now. Perfectionists stay caught in Romans 7, never able to internalize the truth of the next chapter: "Therefore, there is now no condemnation for those who are in Christ Jesus" (Rom. 8:1). They don't have enough grace inside to experience forgiveness.

Good-bad problems are major destroyers. People who can't reconcile either their own or anyone else's faults suffer tremendous isolation because they are unable to attach to real, whole people who are both good *and* bad. The ideals of what "should" be get in the way.

Perfectionists demand that their friends be perfect. Initially, when they click with someone, they will experience a wonderful honeymoon period, full of discoveries about "all the things we have in common" and how "compatible" they are. Then a conflict will arise. They will start to see the other person's faults: they're always late; they don't listen well; they are too controlling. Suddenly the perfectionists are confused and disappointed. Someone they'd believed in, hoped for, expected more from has seriously let them down. And they tend to leave and reenter the fruitless, futile search for the ideal. Since safe people aren't perfect people, they are disqualified, and the perfectionist goes on alone.

In some cases, perfectionists may forgive other people's sins, but be unable to receive forgiveness themselves. Many perfectionists will sabotage potentially good relationships for one reason: being found out. They are afraid to get too close to someone, because their bad self might start leaking out, and the shame and self-condemnation they feel is unbearably painful. Generally, perfectionists opt for isolation rather than to be exposed in their failings. It is sadly ironic that perfectionists shun the very safety that could heal them.

The well-known "commitment-phobic" man is often in this category. He's the type who starts a relationship, gets close, and then disappears. As a single woman friend of mine said after one of these episodes, "I'd understand it if he'd bailed out after a fight. But on our last date, we both started sharing our fears and insecurities. Silly me. I thought that tended to bring people closer together."

What actually happened to the man was just the opposite: He started trusting my friend, and his defenses began slipping. His need for being understood, known, forgiven, and comforted, as Paul talks about (2 Cor. 1:4), was showing. And he couldn't tolerate the risk that his "bad self" would be too bad, too noxious for my friend. So he took the only route he'd taken for years: he ran away.

If you have this good/bad split, you may suffer from depression, "all good or all bad" thinking about yourself or others, anxiety or panic, broken relationships, eating disorders and substance abuse problems, guilt, idealism, inability to tolerate badness, inability to tolerate negative feelings, inability to tolerate weakness, narcissism, perfectionism, rage and anger problems, self-image problems, and sexual addictions.

4. We were not allowed to mature into adults.

Our last developmental need deals with the task of taking on an adult role in life. It is moving from the child's one-down position to the equal and mutual position of being a grown-up.

All of us start off life as an untrained, immature infant. We have unformed values, gifts and talents, emotions and potentials. The primary job of parenting is to help us mature this confusing mass of thoughts and feelings into an adult who is able to function independently.

Being an adult means taking our own roles in life. Developing specialties and expertise in our jobs and careers. Taking on our gender and sexuality roles. Coming to terms with what we believe about life, relationships, God, finances, and all the complex issues of life.

How can we be sinned against in our need to become adults? Here are some ways:

One-up relationships: others who treat us as if we were children
One-down relationships: others who treat us as if we were parents
Control: others who need to be in charge of our lives
Criticism: others who attack when we challenge their thinking

When our emerging adultness is disrupted, we encounter breakdowns in functioning. For example, some people become compliant, obsessive, rule-bound individuals. Some react and become domineering, controlling, parental-types themselves. And some become rebellious, resisting authority figures long beyond their teenage years. None of these positions solve the problem of becoming a grown-up. They are compromises in character development.

How does the adult-injured individual suffer from safety problems? In major ways, but the common denominator is this: They are unable to relate to safe people because safe people encourage adultness. They tend to bring out the best in us, because love "believes all things" (1 Cor. 13:7 NASB). And that's risky. Because we might just start acting like the adult our friends see inside us.

In other words, the adult-injured person is terrified of moving out of the child role, mainly because they were repressed by authority figures and fear criticism. Even though they resent authority, they are afraid of challenging it. And safe relationships create the possibility of a frightening power shift and subsequent conflict.

Bruce, a friend of mine, was part of a successful family business. The operation had been started by his father many years ago, and now he and his brother were the heirs apparent.

The family members worked well together, and the work progressed smoothly. That is, until Bruce's father would subtly put Bruce's ideas down in public and in private. When Bruce, who was quite bright, would generate a new direction for the firm, his father would smile knowingly and actually pat him on the head in a patronizing fashion! This communicated to everyone that Dad still saw his thirty-four-year-old son as a little boy.

Bruce began distancing himself from his family, trying to find a way to get some respect. He developed golfing relationships with some independently-minded businessmen who listened to him as a peer. For the first time in his life, Bruce began feeling like an adult.

Then the roof fell in. Bruce's dad pulled in the reins and basically told him to get back in the family functions and drop his good-for-nothing friends, or he'd be cut off from the family and business both. Obviously, Bruce's dad had sensed his son had started to be a grown-up, and he wasn't about to let that happen.

Sadly enough, it didn't happen. The ultimatum was too soon for Bruce to use his support system to become an adult. So Bruce gave in. He stopped seeing his buddies, stopped bringing up new ideas, and stopped attempting to be a man. He's had bouts of depression since then, but he has been reluctant to get help. Bruce's conflicts in becoming an adult kept him from safety. He was only able to relate to people who treated him like a little boy.

As with the other three areas of development, authority problems can cause a whole host of symptoms, such as anxiety, black-and-white thinking, competitiveness, compulsive behaviors, sexual addiction, substance abuse problems, dependency, depression, fears of disapproval, fears of failure, feelings of inferiority, feelings of superiority, guilt, hatred of authority, idealization of authority, romanticization of childhood, impulse problems and inhibition, needs for approval, judgmentalism, loss of power, need for "permission," no equality between people, rage or passive-aggressive behavior, parenting others, sexual dysfunction, and a "you can't do that" attitude.

Sin in the World

Now that we've seen how we lose safety from both our own sin and that of others, let's broaden our horizons a bit. Let's look at a fallen system that destroys safety.

Have you ever channel surfed through the news on TV and been struck by a world scene of horror and catastrophic loss? You see worldwide ecological problems, another famine in Africa, children orphaned in a senseless war, random acts of violence, and the devastation brought by earthquakes, hurricanes, and volcanoes.

Many of the problems we have now are the direct result of our and others' sin. But there are also grave problems for which we really can't point the finger. There is no specific "perpetrator." It's simply the fact that we now live in a world that also suffers the effects of the Fall. Bad things happen. Planes crash for no reason. Good people can't have children. Earthquakes, tornadoes, and floods take life and love away. Creation itself is in great pain; it "groans and suffers" (Rom. 8:22 NASB). It is in prison: in "bondage to decay" (Rom. 8:21). Disasters, sickness, and death disrupt our lives and destroy our safety.

My friend Nancy had her mother living at home with her and her husband and their four-year-old daughter, Chrissie. Chrissie and her grandmother became very close, and the little girl followed her beloved grandmother everywhere.

Suddenly, Grandma died from an unexpected illness. Chrissie became withdrawn, stopped smiling, and lost weight. Normally quite active, the little girl became listless and passive.

Nancy took her daughter to a child therapist, who diagnosed her as suffering from a depression related to the loss of her grandmother. Part of her heart had resided with Grandma, and she was isolated and in mourning. It took time, but gradually Chrissie's heart began to heal.

Like Chrissie, our safety may have been challenged by death itself. Think for a minute about a cherished friend or relative you have lost to death. Depending on how young you were, how important the person was to you, and your other resources, you might have lost some of the ability to reach out, to trust, and to find safe people. A deep part of the heart might have felt, "If I love again, I'll lose again. It's better to stay apart." Sometimes we can live all our lives under that cloud of loss.

We also lose safety through situations like career moves and financial changes that remove us from loved ones. Factors such as working mothers, single-parent homes, and breakdowns in the family structure contribute to safety losses as well.

Even our very genetic makeup is corrupted by the Fall. For example, some research is pointing to built-in, constitutional tendencies toward problems such as obesity, alcoholism, and homosexuality. Here are problems we inherit from our very DNA—a striking example of the broken system in which we live. These problems remind us of our brokenness: "Behold, I was brought forth in iniquity, and in sin my mother conceived me" (Ps. 51:5 NASB).

God may have dealt you a problematic hand of DNA. In despair and anger, you may have wanted to give up. But even though the pain isn't your fault, it's your responsibility to deal with your problem, rather than to succumb to it. Instead of disconnecting from

God, and rather than giving in to the problem, go to God and his people. God wants us to share our struggles with each other and encourage each other. And God will bless you for doing your best with what you have.

Satan's Strategies

When we look at all the ways we have lost—and still lose—safety, it's easy to overlook our very active and alive enemy, Satan, who works to keep us away from the safe relationships we so desperately need. He has done much damage with three primary tactics: by accusing, tempting, and sifting.

Accusing

Satan has made a profession of trying to have us condemned before God's throne. In fact, the word *Satan* actually means "accuser." For example, he tried to accuse Job (1:9–11) and the nation of Israel (Zech. 3:1) in order to bring judgment upon them.

Satan endlessly tries to separate God from us by reminding him of our guilt. However, God is fully aware of our failings and has made provision for them in the death of Christ. So, in effect, God responds to the accusations by saying to Satan, "Yes, they sinned. But the penalty has been paid. They go free."

Satan doesn't shake God up in the least. Our own response to our guilty state, however, can cause us to lose safety. When we experience the wrong sorts of guilt and shame feelings, our first response is to avoid relationships. We hide, rather than seek love and forgiveness. And the Adversary wins. Anytime you and I take our accused behaviors, emotions, and thoughts into isolation, we are cut off from the safe relationships that could help us deal with the problems.

Tempting

People often think the Devil tries to influence people to do "bad things." While this is true, the demonic strategy is also much deeper. He tries to tempt us to get our needs met without relationship and without humility, the way he wanted to in the beginning.

That's why Jesus' temptation is a model for us. Satan tried to influence him to create food, test God's provision for him, and worship him (Matt. 4:1–11). The theme in all three temptations revolves around Jesus' meeting his needs on his own terms, and not in God's way.

Recently, a good friend named Anne called me at home late at night. She was in crisis, with husband, family, and job problems. It was evident that these weren't new struggles, and I asked her why she hadn't called months ago.

"Oh, you know me," Anne told me. "I try to handle things myself without bothering people. Guess it caught up with me." Anne had, in effect, given in to the first temptation of Jesus by Satan. She had tried to make bread out of stones. Instead of calling a friend, she had depended on her own competence, and it had failed her.

Be aware that when you're hurting, a voice may tell you, "Why bother others? They'll see how weak you are. Where's your faith?" It may be an idea planted by the Tempter to keep you from safe people.

Sifting

Finally, the Devil delights in keeping people away from other people. He knows that the power of love is in relationship. And he is dedicated to our being cut off from God and each other.

After the Last Supper, Jesus told the disciples that Satan had requested permission to "sift you as wheat" (Luke 22:31). "Sifting" refers to splitting up, breaking up, or sorting out. In other words, the Devil wanted the very opposite of Jesus, who desired for us to "be one as we are one" (John 17:22). He wants division, not oneness, because he is very aware of the power of relationship over isolation. He wants to divide and conquer.

We see this strategy sometimes working in the church today. People with emotional issues come to Christians for help, and they are often told crazy things, like:

Get your act together first.
If you had more faith, you wouldn't have this problem.
It's a moral problem.
Don't disrupt the church.

These attitudes keep those who need help "sifted" away from God's own resources, and the body becomes split up and fragmented.

We need the opposite. We need confession of problems, failings, and struggles to be the norm, not the exception. In this way, we become the "two or three" who guarantee that he is in our midst (Matt. 18:20).

Conclusion

There are four ample answers to the question, "How did I lose safety?" We lost it through:

- sin by us
- sin against us
- sin in the world
- Satan's strategies

When we become aware of all the odds stacked against us, maybe a better question is, "How did I not lose even more safety?"

Become a student of yourself. Find which of these areas has hurt you the most and in what ways. Begin working on the problems that have disconnected you. Remember, more than anything, God wants to have you fully reconciled with himself and his people. Jesus' prayer of being "one" applies also to you.

PART TWO

Do I Attract Unsafe People?

CHAPTER FIVE

Do I Have a "Safety Deficit"?

MY FAMILY WENT on a summer vacation when I (John) was about twelve. The six of us traveled to a mountain retreat to enjoy the scenery and activities. One afternoon, we all climbed up to the top of a large hill to view the landscape.

On the way down the steep hill, my ten-year-old sister, Lynn, began running faster and faster, until she was out of control. Disaster loomed at the bottom of the hill. A long stretch of barbed wire fencing straddled the incline, and Lynn was headed right toward it, terrified, trying to stop, but taking longer and longer strides. I can still see her thin, white legs pinwheeling crazily down the steep hill.

My father screamed, "Turn, Lynn, turn!" hoping that the change of angle would slow her down. Hearing him, my sister veered to the side and immediately caught her shoulder on the trunk of a large tree on the hillside. She hit hard. The impact spun her around and slowed her down enough to fall down and roll a few feet. She stopped about four feet from the barbed wire.

When we reached Lynn, her side was already turning blue from the bruising she'd received. She was crying and in lots of pain. But she'd missed the wire. Had she run across the fence at her rate of speed, my sister could have been badly cut.

As we tell the story now, we always end with the words, "I never thought we'd be thankful that Lynn ran into a tree!" But we were.

Do I Have Enough Safe People in My Life?

People with unsafe connections are often out of control, like Lynn, but with no tree to stop them. Instead, they have only sharp barbed wire waiting at the bottom—unsafe friends who can badly hurt them if they run into them. What they need, however, are friends who are stable trees that can deflect them from disaster. As King David put it: "Let a righteous man strike me—it is a kindness" (Ps. 141:5).

Many of us live our entire lives surrounded by barbed wire without any trees to break our fall. We try to pick safe, loving, faithful friends and spouses. And over and over again, we become disappointed and discouraged.

God created us to hunger and thirst for love, because love is our fuel. And God uses people to comfort us (2 Cor. 1:4). When we don't have enough safe relationships regularly sustaining us, we can be in real spiritual and emotional trouble. Yet we may not be aware that a lack of safe people is the problem.

Research on athletics shows that when we work out, we need lots of water at short intervals. Otherwise, we risk dehydration, which can be serious. Yet, we often don't feel thirst during exercise. In fact, the thought of water may make us feel nauseous during peak levels. In the same way, you may have acutely low levels of attachment inside. You may be "safety-deficient." And yet you may not know that you're in trouble.

How can you evaluate if you're "safety-deficient," or running low on safe people? Take a look at how you are doing in four areas of your life: relationships, functioning, physical health, and spiritual life.

Relationships

The quality of our important friendships can tell us a great deal about how much safety we are receiving. Use the following questions as a guide to determine this:

    1. Do you tend to be the "giver" in relationships, rather than having a mutual give and take?

2. Do you find that people approach you when they want something from you, and less to simply spend time with you?
3. Is it difficult for you to open up about your real feelings and problems?
4. Is it hard for you to see other people as a source of emotional and spiritual support?
5. Do you prefer to be alone to deal with your problems?
6. Have you become aware of a pattern in which things are okay when you're not disclosing yourself, but that people withdraw from you when you are honest about yourself?
7. Do you feel that God is the only person who really knows and loves all of you?
8. Do you find yourself choosing people who invariably let you down over time?
9. Are intimate, vulnerable, two-way conversations with others more of a rarity than a regular event?
10. Do you find most of your personal connections revolving more around activities than relationships?

If you can identify with several of these questions, you may have some safety deficiencies in your life. Depending on your own personality structure and style, you'll experience safety lacks in a variety of ways.

Functioning

How about your functional life? Work, activity, fun, and recreation are all about functioning. Many active, busy, productive people are surprised to find that their functioning levels have dropped for no apparent reason. This is often safety-related.

"Monday blues" is a good example. Everyone who's ever worked knows the feeling of dread and lack of motivation that accompanies a return to the office after the weekend. Most of the time we explain Monday blues by contrasting the drudgery of work with the relief of weekends.

Sometimes this is true. Often, however, people go from Friday to Sunday without any relational ties or connections. They may go to church, play softball, ski, or work around the yard—but with nary a soul-to-soul time of intimacy. This certainly wasn't God's intent when he instituted the Sabbath rest. Connection was a vital part, as when Jesus worshiped in community with others on the Sabbath (Luke 4:16).

In other words, Monday blues isn't always about how bad work is. It may be about how depleted we are from the lack of intimacy in our lives.

Another sign of safety deficits is difficulty in completing tasks. Have you ever looked at the pile of projects on your desk or around the house and thought, "Might as well torch the lot of it. I'll never get it all done."

Generally speaking, the first solution that comes to mind is discipline and organization. Get it scheduled out. Plan the time. Stick with it. And often, discipline does help. Just as often, however, our safety deficits sabotage our ability to get things done.

Why? Because of how God constructed us. We can't be finishers with an empty relational tank, no matter how committed and sincere we are. The fuel to be an aggressive self-starter is often simply not there. Remember, before God gave us our job description of subduing and ruling the earth, he first created us to be in relationship to each other (Gen. 1:27–28).

Here's a partial list of other functioning problems that can have safety deficits at their root:

Lapses in concentration
Inability to think creatively
Inability to take risks
Loss of energy
Motivation problems
Failure to achieve goals

It takes lots of drive and energy to function. And if you're surrounded by the wrong people, you can be seriously hampered in this area.

Physical Health

Over the past few years, research has begun to focus on the close relationship between our minds and our bodies. This research simply affirms what the Scriptures have been telling us for millennia: that we don't *have* a body—we *are* a body. When David cried out to God in times of trouble, he was in acute physical and emotional pain: "for my bones are in agony, my soul is in anguish" (Ps. 6:2–3). Jesus' agony in Gethsemane caused sweat "like drops of blood" (Luke 22:44).

Like David and Jesus, our physical well-being is also a good barometer of our emotional and spiritual life. In fact, many doctors attribute a high percentage of medical problems to stress and emotions, which can be quite relationship-sensitive. Look at the following list:

chronic headaches
gastrointestinal problems
back pain
susceptibility to viruses
weight issues

Even cancer and life expectancies have been linked to our emotional well-being. We can't ignore the medical signals we may be receiving.

A small town in Pennsylvania named Roseto is a good example of the importance of relationships in our physical well-being. Many years ago, Roseto was populated by Italian immigrants, who developed a reputation for unusually solid and long-lasting personal relationships. People were friends for generations, and they genuinely cared about each other.

Not only was this town known for relationships, it was also famous for long life. The life expectancies of the citizens was significantly greater than that of the rest of the United States. Researchers began to study them to see what was different about these people.

Quickly, the scientists found the most important variable: relationships. The deep interconnectedness between the residents was rare in other parts of the state and country. But there were two more important findings in this long-term study.

First, the inhabitants of Roseto didn't take any better care of themselves physically than anyone else. They ate lots of red meat and fatty foods and smoked and drank as much as any American. Yet they lived much longer!

Second, the town was researched again in the nineties. By then, industrialization had made its mark. People left, new people moved in, and the connections were broken. Longtime residents observed that you no longer knew the people down the street.

And guess what? As the connections disintegrated, life expectancies took a plunge. Just in case you were thinking of moving to Roseto, think again. Your chances of living longer there are no better than living anywhere else in the country.

What a striking example of how safe people can make a measurable difference in our physical lives!

Spiritual Life

Finally, a lack of safe people can wreak havoc in your personal relationship with God. In fact, your "relational condition" and your "spiritual condition" are as intricately connected as strands on a rope.

This is a major problem, and a very real one. We often learn about the divine from the fleshly. As John writes, "If anyone says, 'I love God,' yet hates his brother, he is a liar. For anyone who does not love his brother, whom he has seen, cannot love God, whom he has not seen" (1 John 4:20). Unsafe people beget a picture of an unsafe God.

Contrary to what some people say, our walk with God isn't an unshakable path, which cannot be affected by others. Others matter a great deal in how safe we feel with the Lord. Many people have lost intimacy with the Savior through believers who wounded them in his name. As Job said: "For the despairing man there should be kindness from his friend; lest he forsake the fear of the Almighty" (Job 6:14 NASB). Have you ever been turned away from your fear of the Almighty by unkind friends? You're not alone.

Think for a minute about your own journey with God. Most of us will remember periods of closeness and warmth, times of doubt or anger, and times when God seemed critical, dangerous, or even apathetic. Draw a simple timeline of your spiritual journal. Briefly identify and describe the stages you've experienced in your walk with God over the years (or months or weeks).

Now draw another timeline under that, and ask the same thing about your closest relationships. Are there parallels in the two journeys? Often, people find that in seasons of life when they felt they belonged to God, they also belonged to good people. And when God felt unsafe, so were the people. These two principles need to always be seen in relation to each other. Never evaluate your spiritual life without also looking at your life in the world.

In summary, safety deficits can cut us off from a vital arm of God's resources—his people. And they can also cut us off from closeness with God himself.

CHAPTER SIX

Why Do I Choose Unsafe Relationships?

R OGER WAS DISILLUSIONED with relationships. He sat in my office telling me that he had about "had it" with people. "You know," he said, "I think I am just going to do the 'me and Jesus' thing for a while. I can't go through another bad relationship. It seems that every time I make a really close friend, I get screwed."

"What happened?" I asked.

"Well, I became friends with Tom when he was on the down and out. His wife had left him, and he had been fired from his job. So, wanting to be helpful, I took him in and nursed him back to health. In the process, we became pretty good friends, or so I thought. I began to trust him, and I told him some personal stuff about struggles I had been having with my family.

"Well, when he got back on his feet, he totally turned against me when I wouldn't agree with everything he was doing. Just because I disagreed with him on how he wanted to organize his business and deal with his former partners, he completely turned against me and started going around town telling people that I had done all sorts of terrible things.

"You wouldn't believe it. I run into people that I hardly know, like today at an attorney's office, and they say things like 'I can't believe what you did to Tom.' And then they will turn and walk away. My name is mud all over town, and I really did nothing but try to help him. Look at what it got me." He looked dazed.

When I asked him further about it, he said that this was not the first time that he had been betrayed by a close friend. In fact, every one of his close friends had ended up betraying him in some significant fashion. "Why can't I at least find one good friend that will not betray me?" Roger asked me.

Why Can't I Find Safe People?

Whenever we speak about the importance of relationships to emotional healing and spiritual growth, someone will always ask the question, "Where are all these safe people you talk about?" They seem to think there are no good people in the world. The real problem, however, is that they are unable to choose safe people.

Why is it that we do not see who is safe and who is not? How is it that some people seem to have a talent for picking destructive people? Whether in friendship or romance, they seem to always end up getting close to people who hurt them. Are they just unlucky? Are their bad relationships all a result of pure chance?

We do not think so. Although there are instances where innocent people are truly betrayed, when a person has a pattern of being hurt by relationships, it is usually not by chance. When people find themselves in destructive relationship after destructive relationship, they must finally decide that the common denominator connecting all those "bad" people is themselves.

But for us to realize that we are the problem is rare. When we have a series of bad relationships, we usually think—as Roger did—that people are just not trustworthy. We get very disillusioned about relationships in general and want to give up. Because we have a tendency to see the problem as outside of ourselves, we think of how bad the other person is.

But in Matthew 7:3–5, Jesus tells us: "Why do you look at the speck of sawdust in your brother's eye and pay no attention to the plank in your own eye? How can you say to your brother, 'Let me take the speck out of your eye,' when all the time there is a plank in your own eye? You hypocrite, first take the plank out of your own eye, and then you will see clearly to remove the speck from your brother's eye."

Here, Jesus ties our focusing on others' faults to our own problems in "seeing." Often we do not face what is getting in the way of our being able to evaluate people: our own character issues. Many of our poor relationships are *our* fault! That's what we will address in this chapter: the character flaws that cause us to pick unsafe people.

We pick unsafe people because we have not come to grips with our own problems. Jessie illustrates this principle beautifully. One day, in a group therapy session, she declared, "This time I am going to do better. I have been married to nine different men, all of them abusive."

"No, you haven't!" exclaimed another woman in the group. "You have been married to the same man with nine different names."

Jessie was startled, but slowly she realized that although her husbands were all different, all of them had the same tendency to hurt her. One may have been openly violent, another passively withdrawn, another sharply critical. But they all lacked the ability to give her the love for which she longed.

So, in order to change, Jessie had to learn that something about her own makeup required or allowed her to make these bad choices in men.

Proverbs 4:23 says that we must "Keep thy heart with all diligence; for out of it are the issues of life" (KJV). From our heart flow the issues that we keep finding ourselves caught up in. If we find that we have recurring dynamics in our lives, such as hurtful relationships with people, then we must look first to ourselves to see what in our hearts causes such things to happen.

Let's look at some of the character flaws that cause us to pick unsafe people.

Inability to Judge Character

One of the chief reasons that we pick destructive people is that we are unable to judge character. Many times, when we are choosing important people in our lives, we do not think of character as the main factor. We look at how we feel, to whom we are attracted, or what seems to "pull" us towards a certain person. Our choices are very subjective.

In a sense, matters of the heart are mostly subjective and unconscious, and that's not bad. Soul connections should not always be made on a rational basis. What a boring life that would be! The unconscious part of ourselves has a wisdom of its own, and in some ways our heart knows what it wants and needs. That is valid.

But God has made us with two sides of our being, the rational and the emotional; when they are in conflict, we are in trouble.

We need to use both reason and emotion in our choosing of people. We get into danger when we ignore our reason, when we find our hearts are attracted to people that our heads "know better" than to choose. At those times, we find ourselves picking people who cannot satisfy our needs and whose character does not measure up to our essential values. *Our hearts become disconnected from our values and in conflict with our true needs.* Because our hearts have been programmed to seek some sort of sickness inside, we find relationships that match the sickness inside our hearts. For example, many single Christians find themselves falling head over heels in love with someone who is unloving or irresponsible.

Jesus warns us to face first what is inside our hearts, and only then will we be able to judge others accurately and pick safe relationships. Our own character issues blind us to the destructiveness of other people. We must first realize that we have a problem in being able to judge character before we can stop playing the naive victim.

Isolation and Fear of Abandonment

Our lack of connection is a big reason why we choose unsafe people. If we are not able to connect in an intimate way with others, then we will often pick people who are unable to connect as well. If someone is isolated inside, she will pick isolating relationships until she addresses her own problem.

Fear of abandonment fuels an ongoing isolating connection. Many times someone who is in a painful relationship should set strong disciplinary boundaries or cut off the relationship altogether (Matt. 18:17; 1 Cor. 5:11–13) for a time. But he fears being alone so much that he can't do it. Every time he thinks of standing up to the other person, or getting out of the relationship, he is overwhelmed by feelings of loss and aloneness, and he either avoids taking the difficult step to begin with, or he quickly caves in. Because he doesn't have primary safe and supportive relationships, he would rather have the unsafe relationship than nothing at all. This all-or-nothing split keeps the isolation and the abandonment going.

Defensive Hope

Defensive hope is hope that protects us against grief and sadness. Sometimes simply hoping a person will change keeps us from the pain that we need to face. Humans are incredible optimists when it comes to destructive relationships. For some reason we think that a person who is hurtful, irresponsible, out of control, abusive, or dishonest is going to change if we just love them correctly or more or enough. We think that if we just let them know about their mistakes, or cry the blues, or get angry, that they will change.

In short, we have hope, but it is hope that disappoints. In this scenario we use hope to defend ourselves against facing the truth about someone we love. We do not want to go through the sadness of realizing that they probably are not going to change. We don't want to accept the reality about who they are. So, we hope.

Usually this kind of hope did not start in our current relationship. We usually have an old pattern of not facing grief and disappointments in many past relationships, dating back to childhood.

Facing sadness is difficult, for it places the responsibility for change on us, instead of hoping that the unsafe person is going to change. We have to learn to not expect that he will change. We have to make other friends. We have to adapt to a nonfulfilling marriage. We have to get the courage to set limits and consequences and make many more tough choices that may change our relationships.

Yes, hope is easier in the beginning, but in the end it is more difficult. Not facing reality is to stay stuck and to get more of the same in the future. Defensive hope is one of the biggest reasons that we allow destruction to continue in life.

Unfaced Badness

Joe was a super saint. He was one of the most responsible people everyone knew. He was faithful in his walk with God, very giving to other people, morally pure, and all the things that a "good Christian" is supposed to be. But, he had a string of "bad girl" relationships. He was very attracted to women who were quite the opposite of him: women who were impulsive, irresponsible, morally loose, and generally immature.

Joe had a tendency to be "holy" and be irresistibly drawn to "unholy" people. The problem is that neither Joe, nor anyone else, is completely holy (Mark 10:18). We all have bad parts that we need to own and confess (1 John 1:10). If we do not own our own badness, we will often hook up with others for help in keeping the illusion alive that the badness is outside of us, in someone else.

Many people choose "unsafe relationships" because they have not faced their own badness and are finding it vicariously in someone else. This dynamic is very familiar to parents whose "good" teenager hooks up with a total loser. Unconsciously, the teenager is trying to bring the split polarities together. When the family begins to own its badness, the teenager will not have to go somewhere else to find some.

Merger Wishes

Susie was in love. She sat in my office and ecstatically told me of the new man in her life. Neal was everything that she had ever wanted, and she felt like she had never felt before. He was financially successful and well-respected in the business community where she worked. He was one of the leaders in the singles ministry at her church. He had all of the polish to which she had always been attracted. Strong and aggressive, Neal seemed to be able to master any situation.

But as I asked her more and more about the relationship, I discovered that her new relationship did not have much substance. When I asked her about how she and Neal relate, she would start to talk all over again about who he was and what image he projected. "He does this, or he knows so and so, or he has one of those," Susie said. But Neal did not seem to show real interest in her as a person. He seemed to be using her as an object to bolster his picture of himself. (Susie was very attractive.) In reality, she was more of a hood ornament than a person to him.

But when I tried to point out some of this to her, she would have none of it. She could not see that they were not building a strong relationship. I could see that when all the excitement wore off she was going to be a very empty person.

What was she doing? Psychologists call it a *merger wish*. She was trying to make up for the things she felt she lacked inside by fusing her identity with Neal. Susie's family was poor, and her father was passive and not very successful. By merging her identity with

Neal's, Susie felt like she could make up for all the shame she felt about herself and her background. His image, his money, his standing in the community and the church—these were all things that she had always admired in others but had never felt she could have for herself. Now, through Neal, she could become a part of all those things.

There were other reasons behind Susie's merger wish. Neal was aggressive and strong, able to assert himself in the world. Being strong and standing up to people was difficult for Susie, as was making a successful life for herself in the career world. She covered up for her lack of assertion by being loving and kind to others, giving to her friends so they would like her. The thought of learning how to become more assertive and stand up to strong people frightened her to death. She hated conflict.

So, with a strong man by her side, all of her problems were solved. She did not have to learn to be a strong person; she had one. She did not have to learn how to formulate goals and pursue them; he did. With him by her side, she had done everything, without even having to.

The seduction of a "merger" is that someone tries to achieve her spiritual and life growth goals without doing the difficult work. But in reality this pattern blinds us to the flaws in other people's character and can lead to many destructive choices.

Fear of Confrontation

Andrea also had a pattern of choosing unsafe friends. She always had a close friend who did many good things for her, but who also consistently hurt her. Her current friend, Sandra, cared about Andrea and was intelligent and responsible, but she had a critical spirit.

Andrea was often in turmoil over some judgmental thing Sandra had said, because Sandra acted as though she knew best how to run Andrea's spiritual life and well-being. Andrea could have told Sandra to mind her own business, or she could have just accepted her for the parental type that she was and not let her affect her.

But Andrea did not do any of those. She tried and tried to live up to Sandra's approval standards and fretted when she could not. Finally she sought counseling. When I asked her what she had tried to do, she said, "Nothing, really. I mean, I do the best I can to please her."

"But have you ever told her how you feel when she is so critical?" I asked.

"You must be kidding. I could never talk to Sandra that way!" She almost seemed astonished that anyone would even consider confronting Sandra.

"Why couldn't you just tell her that you like her a lot and still want to be friends, but that you experience her as critical, and you would appreciate it if she would give specific advice or evaluation only when you ask for it?" I said.

Andrea was not ready to do what I suggested, but we began to explore the issue of why something so simple was so difficult for her. The more we talked about it, the more she could see that confronting critical people had always been a problem for her and had gotten her into several very hurtful relationships in the past. When she would be with someone who was critical or hurtful, she was unable to talk with them about it and resolve the pattern.

The problem with the inability to confront people is that nonconfronters are the exact kind of people that hurtful people end up with. It is like a duck finding water. People who have good boundaries, who are able to confront others clearly, and who resolve problems in their relationships do not have the kinds of hurtful dynamics that Andrea experienced over and over. They are able to handle hurtful, unsafe people through biblical confrontation. But if someone is unable or afraid to do that, they are literally set up for a pattern of unsafe relationships, and they will rarely find a safe relationship.

The inability to confront is license for unsafety. Being unable to confront someone is like having a farm with no fences, or a body without skin. No matter how careful one is, he would always be getting poisoned or infected because of the lack of protection. Someone who is afraid to confront hurtful or abusive patterns in a relationship will find plenty of unsafe people available to take advantage of him.[1]

---

[1] For more help with confrontation, see *Boundaries* (Grand Rapids: Zondervan, 1992).

Romanticizing

Romanticizing is an idealized way of looking at someone or some situation, in which the romanticizer only sees the good and omits a big part of reality. She ignores the person's faults, or worse yet, she turns them into strengths by viewing them romantically. A romanticizer may even idealize the strength and aggression of an abuser, admiring how an abusive person can stand up to people, and not seeing his hurtful actions.

Chris romanticized in her relationships. She was dating a very irresponsible man. She saw his scatteredness as spontaneity, his lack of structure as creativity, his inability to hold down a consistent job as being too intelligent for all his bosses, his spendthrift habits as a lack of concern for temporal things like money and financial security. She was able to take all his glaring problems and fall in love with them, seeing them in a totally unrealistic, idealized way.

People who are perpetually caught up in the romantic have set themselves up to meet many unsafe people. "Charm is deceitful," says the Bible. Real relationships get past romantic feelings to true love and true intimacy. But romanticizers do not want reality, because it has always disappointed them in the past. Romantics often cover up for a great deal of disappointment in their own personal history and idealize the future to make up for the sadness they have denied in their past. But we always return to what is denied in us, and the romantic finds the sadness that he or she has denied. But the problem is that they find it not in their own souls, where it could be worked out, but in new relationships. Desperately wanting to avoid painful reality, they create new painful realities with every new romanticized unsafe person.

Need to Rescue

Jerry felt so strongly about Mindy that he could hardly describe it. "I have never felt such a deep connection with anyone. I just can't let her go."

Unable to leave a relationship that had been very hurtful to him over five years, Jerry pleaded with his friends for help. But they did not know what to say to him anymore. They had heard all the stories of how difficult Mindy was to be around, how impossible it was to please her no matter what he did, and how intense she was about insignificant things. Whenever they told him that he should say good-bye, he would have the same answer: the connection was too strong.

He came to counseling to try to get out of the relationship because he could not do it by himself. We talked about the strong connection he felt. As it turned out, Jerry felt most connected when they would break up, and she would be really sad, or when other terrible things would befall her, and she would need him to comfort her or help her out. In fact, the best times they had were when she needed consoling, or help, or money, or some other crisis intervention by him.

The truth was that they did not really have a mature connection at all. They had a rescuing connection. When she was in pain or in need of help, they were close. Other times, things were stormy.

As we worked together, Jerry realized that he was a rescuer. He picked people who couldn't meet any of his needs because they were so needy themselves. He would then step in and rescue them.

Jerry had learned the rescuing pattern early in life from a needy mother who was unable to be satisfied. No matter what he or his father did, it was never enough. And with all of his mother's crises, he learned to feel the closest when he was stepping in and taking care of her. It was his deepest connection with her. And now he had found the same sort of connection with someone else who needed rescuing. So he was unable to leave.

People who need rescuing are not taking responsibility for their life. And people who do not take responsibility for their life are not safe, even though they may be very nice. Ultimately, they are not growing, and they are not fostering growth in the people who are rescuing them. Their life has spurts of sentimentality, but not a lot of mature love. Because a rescuer needs an unsafe person to rescue, rescuing always leads to unsafe people in one's life.

Familiarity

"I don't want to move out of hell, because I know the names of all the streets," Tammy said in jest. She knew that she had some hurtful relational patterns, but to change them was going to be very hard work. "Wouldn't it be easier to stay like I am?" she would ask from time to time. And my reply would always be the same: "Tammy, has it been easy through the years?" And then she would get back to work.

Tammy was one of those people who seemed addicted to hurtful relationships. No sooner would she get through with one than she would find another. She went from one self-centered man to another. Although they seemed different on the outside, they all had the same pattern of relating to her. She would be emotionally responsible for them and live to make them happy. They were all little boys inside, who needed someone to make them feel like they were powerful men. And Tammy would do that. She would idealize them, worship them, and listen to their stories of how they were never wrong and everyone else had done them in.

As we began to explore this pattern, we discovered that all these men were very much like her own father. Her father was a very narcissistic man who needed the whole family to think he was great, and Tammy played the role of cheerleader well. She never said no to him and lived to make him feel special. When he would exaggerate his accomplishments or minimize his faults, they would all keep quiet, and Tammy's mom would explain it away, making him sound all the better for it.

So, Tammy was doing what was familiar. She had simply learned this pattern of relating from her father, modeled it with her mother, and continued it through three marriages. It was not something that she had to think about; it just happened. And that is the way that the familiar happens—without trying.

God has designed us to learn patterns of relating in our family of origin. In his plan, we should be learning honesty, responsibility, and love, and then teaching them to our children. But when families model other ways of relating, children learn those as well. And Tammy did precisely that. She learned some sick ways of relating, they became familiar, and she repeated them.

Like Tammy, we will always pick what is familiar—until we develop a new familiar.

Victim Role

A victim is someone who has no power. Things are done to them, not by them. For instance, if you are run over by a drunk driver as you cross the street, you are a victim. A child who is sexually abused is a powerless victim against an adult. Such people are powerless and do not have any choice.

A victim role, however, is a pattern of relating and behaving that an adult does who actually is not powerless anymore, but experiences himself as such and acts out that powerlessness in his situations and relationships. He plays a role in being victimized, and does not make the choices that are available to him to keep that from happening.

Victims do not see themselves as actors or agents—they see themselves as acted upon. They use victim language.

- "We ended up in bed" instead of "I chose to sleep with."
- "I had to" instead of "I chose to."
- "My taxes were late because the accountant didn't finish them in time" instead of "I was so late getting my information to the accountant that my taxes were late."

Victims do not take responsibility for their choices and behaviors. They see themselves as reacting to some power greater than them, be it traffic, the weather, a person, the economy, God, or luck.

Victims are prime candidates for unsafe people. Unsafe people who take advantage of victims are called perpetrators, people who seek and destroy victims to gratify themselves. To the extent that someone will not take responsibility for their choices, perpetrators will "make" choices for them. The victim passively gives the reins of his life to someone else. And turning one's choices over to perpetrators is very "unsafe." Victims need to learn that to not choose is to make a choice, and that they can take more control of their relationships than they believe by, for example, setting boundaries against abusive behavior and sticking to them.

Guilt

Guilt also causes people to get involved with unsafe people. People who carry guilt will look for someone to play the guilt inducer in their life. The "guilt inducer" often plays the martyr role, acting like his misery is the fault of the person who feels guilty. The guilty party, in turn, is hooked into taking responsibility for the other person's pain or anger or disappointments. He is easily manipulated and never feels free in the relationship.

The hook, however, lies within the person who picks the guilt inducer. She will feel as if the guilt is "put on her," or so and so "makes me feel guilty." But this thinking is a disavowal of responsibility. *For someone to make us feel guilty, we have to have some part of us that gets hooked into that dynamic and agrees with the accuser.* This is why the power to be free is within us. When we begin to deal with our guilt, we can get free of the hook that guilt inducers use to control us.

People who feel loved by others and understand their freedom and lack of condemnation in Christ (Rom. 8:1) evaluate messages from others in terms of love and whether or not they are really at fault. If they are at fault, then they act appropriately. If they are not, then they have the personal boundaries required to not take the guilt hook, and to let the other party bear responsibility for his own feelings and choices (Prov. 19:19). If someone's unsafe relationships center around the dynamic of guilt, she needs to find the source of the guilt within her own personality makeup and work on changing that critical voice inside. Then the inducers will have no foothold with which to manipulate her.

Perfectionism

Tom was a perfectionist. He would not really think of himself as such, as he was not particularly compulsive about details and nit-picky the way that a lot of perfectionists are. But he was perfectionistic in that he wanted others to always think well of him. If they did not see him as ideal in whatever context he was in, he was subject to anxiety and would begin to perform to meet the ideal expectations of the one he was with.

Tom's perfectionism propelled him toward people who demanded perfection in others. In this way, he could find an external match for the perfectionistic voice in his own head. He usually struggled with this dynamic in his work life, trying to please bosses that could never be pleased. The dynamic would sometimes interfere in his value system as well, as he would make compromises to portray the ideal image he wanted to portray. For example, he would often overspend in order to impress people.

Finally Tom's perfectionism wore him down. He joined a group that was able to show him that the hurtful relationships in which he got involved resulted from his choosing people who put the perfectionistic pressure on him that he put on himself. As he was able to allow good people to love and accept him as he really was, then the power of those that would not accept him disappeared. He no longer was drawn to people who made perfectionistic demands on him. And he stopped trying to live up to the perfectionistic demands of his wife, which forced her to deal with her own disappointments instead of making him responsible for all the problems in their marriage. As he changed, so did she, breaking free of the unsafe role she had played in his life.

Repetition

We spoke earlier in this chapter about Jessie, a woman who had picked nine unsafe husbands. She had more than one reason for doing that, but one of them is called repetition—she was caught in a destructive relational pattern that she had learned early in life and had repeated over and over again. Although the pattern was not satisfying or growth producing, Jessie repeated her behavior without learning anything from her mistakes. She did not change, and her next relationship was no closer to health than the last one.

When we are very young, patterns of relating are "hard-wired" into our brains as part of our character. We have certain dynamics and patterns that we repeat until we change them. For Jessie, the pattern was

1. feel attracted and excited by an emotionally unavailable man
2. experience his stimulating come-and-go game as "being in love"
3. experience his hurtful behavior as creating more longing in her
4. begin to try to "win" him over by compliant behavior
5. he gets more self-centered the more compliant she gets
6. gets so painful that she can no longer stand it
7. tries to break up
8. is unable to stand the separation so she returns to the relationship
9. repeats the cycle

As Jessie began to understand her pattern, she could see that it was the same pattern she had learned with her mother. Her mother had been volatile and difficult to connect with and often left her needing more. Jessie would try to placate her mom with good behavior, but it was never enough. Anger in another person was something she tried to perform her way through instead of confront and deal with. So the pattern was set—this was how her mind was programmed to deal with relationships. There was no wiring for anything else. So she repeated the pattern over and over the way that a rat runs down a familiar maze.

Jessie had to gain insight into the pattern, deal with her unresolved feelings toward her mother, learn how to connect with satisfying people, and then make some tough choices and learn new behaviors. In that way, her repetition ceased, and she was able to find new kinds of relationships.

This is an appropriate place to correct a common misunderstanding about relationships. Often it is said that if you have trouble with a man in a friendship or relationship, you are repeating patterns learned with your father. If you have trouble with a woman, you are "dealing with your mother." This is not true. Patterns of relating are patterns of relating, and although there are specific reactions we have to specific same-sex or opposite-sex interactions, our problematic relational patterns can certainly cross gender lines. For example, an unfinished pattern with a mother can affect how we relate to men friends who have her same personality. What is important is the dynamic, and the resulting behavior and feeling patterns that are repeated.

Denial of Pain and Perceptions

Hebrews 5:14 says, "But solid food is for the mature, who because of practice have their senses trained to discern good and evil" (NASB). The root word for *practice* also can mean "habit" and comes from the word meaning "echo." In other words, we should learn from what we experience over and over.

But people whose senses have been dulled do not learn from experience. They may have had abusive parents who claimed that their abuse was actually loving, or perfectionistic parents who said, "I only want the best for you." Therefore they have learned not to trust their pain, their perceptions, their feelings, and all the other ways that God gave us to discern reality.

People whose senses have been dulled often get stuck in destructive relationship patterns. They have not learned to pay attention to—or they actively deny—their God-given gut feelings that someone is hurting them. They cannot discern good from evil. And so over and over again they find themselves entangled in evil, destructive relationships.

Our feelings, intuition, and perceptions are important. It is very important for us to get in touch with our feelings instead of just believing what someone tells us—especially when that person may be unsafe. Instead, we should test and develop our perceptions with safe people, Scripture, our support group, or our therapist. With their help, we should discern the fruits of our relationships. Then we will mature, learning from our experiences instead of repeating them ad infinitum. As 1 Thessalonians 5:21–22 advises: "Test everything. Hold on to the good. Avoid every kind of evil."

A Necessary Part of Sanctification

There are many reasons that we pick unsafe people. And it's good for us to look at those reasons, for they are all essential issues of the spiritual life that the Bible commands us to look at anyway. Look at the list again: inability to judge character, isolation, false hope, unfaced badness, merger wishes, fear of confrontation, romanticizing, rescuing, familiarity, victim roles, guilt, perfectionism, repetition, and denial. These are all issues that the Bible deals with very directly and tells us to face as part of our sanctification process.

It is for this reason that finding safe people is not just a luxury—it's a necessary part of growing spiritually mature. God wants us to have good relationships and to be people who are able to fight evil. If you have a pattern of bad relationships, it may not be the other person's fault but actually be a sign of your own spiritual immaturity.

Look at the list of issues in this chapter and see what applies to you. Recognize your patterns, then change them, and you will begin to grow in the grace and knowledge of the Lord. And as you change, the people around you will adapt and change—and you will break the patterns of behavior that have kept you trapped in unsafe relationships.

As you change your behavior, however, watch out for the false solutions—remedies we often try in our efforts to deal with unsafe relationships. Those false solutions are the subject of the next chapter.

CHAPTER SEVEN

False Solutions

THIS CHAPTER IS DESIGNED to save you a lot of time.

As a novice in the world of computers, I (John) recently bought a software product, took it home, and attempted to install it. Within minutes, I had crashed my entire system.

In deep cyber despair, I called a friend who was a technical expert. After helping me get back on line, he then told me, "When in doubt, read the manual. Especially the parts about what *not* to do."

And that's the intent in this section of the book. We'll try to help you see what hasn't worked for you in your relationships—and save you time so you don't make further mistakes.

Who Qualifies?

Everyone has had relational problems. It's doubtful that you're coming to this book with no cuts or bruises. So, most likely, you'll find some of your unsafe patterns of relating in this chapter. Learn from them. These are the false solutions that don't work in finding safe people. They don't work, and they aren't helpful.

These false answers are much of the reason people begin giving up on love and intimacy. They've tried and tried, and they have failed so many times that they figure "that relational thing must be meant for those relational people." But everyone is created to be relational. So let's read on and learn which potholes to swerve by.

The Seven "Doings"

We'll look at the false solutions as a list of seven "doings." These "doings" are activities and attitudes that seem to promise

111

hope for safe relationships. Yet in reality, they cause conflicts, hurt, and isolation.

1. Doing the Same

The first mistake we make in trying to find safe people is to repeat history. We have a flat learning curve. Failure and pain don't teach us what God intended them to.

Rob and Lu Ann came to see me for premarital counseling. They wanted to prevent any unnecessary problems in their marriage as much ahead of time as possible.

This couple was especially concerned because each had been divorced. The devastation that the split-ups had played in their lives had made them more wary and thoughtful this time around. They were more sober about the marriage, and less idealistic than your average "never-married-early-twenties" pair.

"What have you learned about yourself from the first marriage?" is one of the questions I ask in this case. It helps people understand their character patterns and look at possible pitfalls in the relationship.

When I asked them the question, both Rob and Lu Ann were somewhat perplexed. They'd honestly never considered the issue before. Both of them told me, "Nothing." As we continued exploring, I found out why. Both of them had simply figured they'd married a bad person the first time around, and now they were marrying a good person. Case closed.

So we reopened the case. And, not surprisingly, we found some of the crazy things that had attracted Rob and Lu Ann to their previous mates were still alive and kicking this time around.

For example, Rob was somewhat immature and was drawn to "take-charge" types of women. He liked the fact that they provided stability, structure, and order. His first wife had been highly structured and quite definite in her opinions, to the point of being a controlling person. This control had driven Rob crazy, contributing to the divorce.

Lu Ann had many of the same traits as Rob's ex. Though more loving, she also hid behind structure and efficiency. Lu Ann also had a controlling streak in her.

In her turn, Lu Ann had married a man who was emotionally accessible and loving, but totally irresponsible. He didn't work steadily, pay bills, or carry through on commitments. And, though not as extreme, Rob had some of her ex's characteristics.

Imagine their discomfort as we began to discover that they were engaged to people who were similar to their ex's! Now more aware of the dynamics, however, they did marry, and then they worked hard on the issues.

That's what doing the same is all about. When we don't sit back in an armchair with a cup of coffee after a failure and ask ourselves, "Why?" we're likely to end up in the same place again.

You may be one of those people who's simply been unaware that you've been repeating a pattern of picking poor fits for yourself. For example, some women are drawn to aggressive or controlling men. Some men desire (s)mothering women. Some workers choose critical bosses. And some parishioners pick legalistic churches. The combinations are endless.

Read the signs. Signs are certain truths and evidences that we are to glean information from, in order to prepare ourselves. You may need to take a look at some of the signs that tell you you're stuck in a pattern. Begin asking yourself:

Am I having the same conversations with different people?
Are the problems and conflicts similar, such as abandonment, control, guilt, irresponsibility, rage?
Are my friends telling me there's a problem?
Am I becoming able to predict the end of a relationship?

These are good signs to cue in on. Remember, she who neglects the past is doomed to repeat it.

2. Doing the Opposite

The seventies were an exciting time to be in college. Vietnam, Watergate, Woodstock, and the Jesus Movement were all great reasons to not study. There was always some crisis of ideals and a lot of intelligent people to talk to.

My college friend, Toby, was the sum and substance of all these movements for me. Toby was a fascinating guy. He really did it all.

Over about seven years, I watched Toby's trek across the ideological universe. I'd see him every few months, so the changes were more apparent to me. He was a pastor's son who had had lots of conflicts living up to his dad's ideals for him. Yet he couldn't sit down man-to-man and discuss the differences with his dad because his dad would react in guilt and rage. So Toby was pretty much left to himself in deciding who he was, and what manhood was all about.

Here's a thumbnail sketch of Toby's wanderings:

Gets to college and goes girl-crazy. Different date every night.
Next year, discovers drugs.
Next year, arrested for dealing but not convicted.
Next year, finds God again.
Next year, marries a pastor's daughter.
Next year, evangelizes all his friends and prepares for ministry.
Next year, empties his bank account and drives away in his wife's car.

I've lost touch with any new developments. But the pattern is clear: Toby wasn't maturing. He was reacting. Attempting to work out his issues of love, responsibility, and failure, Toby was making zigzags across the tapestry of his life. And he obviously was causing himself and others a great deal of pain in the process.

Doing the opposite is the second false solution to finding safe people. Many times, we tend to make extreme moves based on our pain and confusion. And many times we end up out of the frying pan and into the microwave.

It's easy to knee jerk when you've been hurt. Here's a brief list of opposites that you may have found yourself encountering:

Falling in love reactively:

someone who is reserved and quiet to someone who is out of control
someone who is isolated to someone who is all emotions
someone who is irresponsible to a control freak

Choosing friends who are opposite from your family of origin:

controlling family—impulsive friends

chaotic family—rigid friends
abusive family—permissive friends

Choosing religious settings in a reactive manner:
liberal to legalistic
overconservative to anti-doctrinal
intellectual theology to experience-based theology

The problem here is, you don't solve the problem. You switch problems. Problems you often have no experience dealing with.

Why do we react in these ways with our important relationships? It's because of a dynamic called *splitting*. When we split, we see one type of relationship as all-good and another as all-bad. It is a black-and-white way of relating to others.

Splitting prevents us from taking in the good someone did for us, and it doesn't allow us to mature. It keeps us in a perpetual relational pinball machine, bouncing from one disaster to another. We idealize someone, get disappointed, then idealize their polar opposite. The exciting-but-irresponsible person is exchanged for the steady-but-boring person.

It's common, for example, for someone to hurt us so badly that we make that individual—and her ilk—something to avoid. In that way, we hope to never have to relive the pain they caused us again. But then we neglect to integrate the good and godly qualities we liked and look for them in the next relationship.

People are more than the sum total of their unsafe traits. Serial killers can help old ladies across the street and be sincere about it. And loving, warm people can have rage attacks. Don't confuse people with their unsafe traits. Instead, learn to identify what traits hurt you. And keep from equating people with their negative traits. They are more than that, though it may not feel like it at the time.

God wants you to learn to wisely discern these matters: "Teach me knowledge and good judgment" (Ps. 119:66). Begin to develop the ability to filter out, discern, and evaluate character.

3. Doing Too Much

Linda sat down in my office, frustrated and confused. She had a history of unsafe relationships, both romantic and platonic, and had been working on the issue.

"I'm giving up on this relationship business," she told me. "I've done everything you're talking about, and I don't get any closer to people."

Now I was confused. Mainly because I'd told Linda lots of things. So I didn't know which "everything" she was discouraged about. "What do you mean?" I asked.

"You said to get involved with people, that I can't learn about connections in a vacuum."

I agreed. "So what's not working?"

She pulled a long list from her purse. "This," Linda said, "is a list I put together of all the involvements I've had in the past few months. And nothing's happening."

I read the list, which looked something like this:

Dancing lessons: ballroom, disco, and line
Sports: sailing, rollerblading, golf, and tennis
Music: opera, modern, and piano lessons
Art: ceramics and museums
Spiritual: Bible study, worship, and missions
Career: Ongoing training, night school to earn an MBA

"What are you grinning at?" Linda asked me. I wasn't even aware I was smiling.

I told her, "This is a proud moment for me. I've never met a real live renaissance woman."

"Now I'm really confused," Linda said.

I explained, "Linda, this is the most well-rounded, comprehensive, and exhausting list I've ever seen. I can't imagine how you can even get up in the mornings. But it's not solving your problem.

"These are all great activities, designed to develop you and help you in your life. But each of them is primarily functional, rather than relational. Their goal is competence in some skill, or recreation, or learning more about God's creation. But relationship isn't the goal. These are 'doing' things, not 'connecting' things."

Linda started to get it. "You know, I've noticed that I am talking to people at these activities. But all the talk is about tennis or management theories. I've wondered when someone in the classroom was going to ask me about my emotional and spiritual life."

"Don't hold your breath," I said.

Safety isn't "by the way." You may have, like Linda, thought that the more things you did, the more people you'd meet. And the more people you'd meet, the better your odds for making relationships. Actually, there's some truth to that. We need to actively seek relationship with God and others. Many people have found healthy friendships on the way to learning waltz steps or golf swings.

However, relationships are more accidental than purposeful with Linda's approach. Most of these people are investing their money, energy, and time for a skill-based or functional reason. So for them, connection is incidental, not a priority. And it may even be something to be avoided.

Which brings us to the deeper issue: many people stay in functional arenas because they are afraid of relationship. Hurt, wary, and avoidant, they would like to get close to others, but not too close. Having a project to work on and talk about provides the semblance of relationship, but without the risk. And that's also what Linda discovered about herself. Her real motive was to stay disconnected, not attached. The renaissance woman was a scared little girl inside.

That's why Jesus explained to Martha that her sister Mary had "chosen what is better" (Luke 10:42). Being close to Jesus was first priority. Task completion is good, but closeness to God and others must always take precedence.

Some relational contexts and activities are designed and intended for fostering closeness. For example, many churches have support groups and relationally oriented Bible studies. They often have the stated purpose of helping people get connected. Check these out, ask people about their experience with them, and try them.

By the way, Linda began dealing with her fears of closeness and got into a good support group. Then it was amazing how uncluttered her "list" became!

4. Doing Nothing

One of the highlights of visiting my hometown in North Carolina is catching up with old friends. I saw an old family friend named Alberta, who'd been close to our family for decades. She had been retired for many years now and was enjoying her rest.

Wondering what she did with her time now, I asked her, "So what have you been doing this year?" Alberta didn't miss a beat.

Rocking in her caneback chair, she smiled and said, " 'Bout what you see me doin' right now."

In other words, taking it easy. Actually, that wasn't true. Alberta was still active in many community and church doings, but she never liked letting on. The picture she was painting for me, however, was one of repose, respite, and "doin' nuthin'."

When you've worked sixty hours a week and raised a family for forty years, it makes sense to slow down. Alberta had completed many of her assignments on earth: "I have fought the good fight, I have finished the race, I have kept the faith" (2 Tim. 4:7). It's time to grab that easy chair, enjoy the view, and take a nap.

But not if you're looking for safe people.

The "Doing Nothing" false solution afflicts many of us who would like to be connected to good relationships. You may be someone who genuinely wants connection—and yet isn't taking any steps to plug in.

Here are some examples of the "doing nothing" approach to finding safe people:

Scheduling your weekly activities—and omitting relationships.

Becoming discouraged because no one calls—and forgetting that your phone can make calls as well as receive them.

Chronically being too exhausted to make contact with others.

Being unable to feel lonely, therefore not making plans to connect (this is a little like avoiding medical checkups until there are chest pains).

So let's say you've identified yourself as a "nothing doer." Why would this happen? There are several reasons.

Some people are simply paralyzed when it comes to taking initiative. They know what they want to do, but they just can't follow through. This condition is called an *aggressive conflict*.

An aggressive conflict is basically an internal war. The war revolves around things like risk-taking, action, making changes, and follow-through. One part of you says, "Go for it!" and another says, "But what if _____ (fill in the blank with a catastrophe) happens?" And more often than not, side two wins out. Better safe than sorry.

Conflicts in aggression have many causes. The bottom line, however, is generally that the individual has been either (1) abandoned or (2) punished for taking initiative. When they've attempted to tell the truth, confront, or try something new, someone has pulled away or been critical. Thus the "better-safe-than-sorry" perspective on life.

Another reason for doing nothing is passivity. Passivity is very different from aggressive conflicts. The passive individual has another kind of internal war. Actually, her "warring" is more like "waiting." The aggressively conflicted person is like a Shelby Cobra revved up to 5000 rpm, but sitting in neutral. The passive individual reminds you of an AMC Gremlin barely idling. They just don't get around to making relational moves.

Passivity comes from different sources, for example:

Being trained to do nothing until someone gives an order.

Having a "do everything" parent who didn't allow you to learn responsibility.

Developing a fantasy life in which you are rescued from your circumstances by others, instead of solving your own problems.

Believing that you are incompetent, and so giving up.

If you find passive leanings in yourself, begin looking at how costly this has been for you. Look at the opportunities missed, people who moved on, and places you never went. This may be painful, but it will help you to start moving out of the "on hold" position in life.

5. Doing for Others

Here's a common mistake which is so often spiritualized away that it goes completely undetected. Have you ever heard some well-meaning saint attempting to be helpful to a struggler, and saying something like, "If you want love, you need to give love. Go find someone who needs help, who's less fortunate, and your cup will be full"? If you haven't heard this, then either you need to get more involved in religious activities or you live on the moon.

The idea here is that in serving, we are blessed. In giving, we receive. And in helping, we are assisted. And, the thinking goes, this principle should also apply to finding safe people. To find relationship, give relationship.

Now, properly understood, this is a biblical principle: "And if you spend yourselves in behalf of the hungry and satisfy the needs of the oppressed, then your light will rise in the darkness, and your night will become like the noonday" (Isa. 58:10). God blesses our blessing. He loves to see his church love the afflicted.

But the problem here is our motive. Motives are important to God, for they help dictate our behaviors: God wants us to give, serve, and help liberally and sacrificially. But not out of emptiness, loneliness, or a need to be loved: "If I give all I possess to the poor and surrender my body to the flames, but have not love, I gain nothing" (1 Cor. 13:3).

Instead, we are to give out of a grateful, overflowing heart: "God loves a cheerful giver" (2 Cor. 9:7). We give cheerfully because we've been given to.

Which leads us to the point: finding safe people is not a search for a ministry, but a search for spiritual survival. It is not an avenue to be useful, but a vital ingredient for growth. And it's easy to confuse the two.

Let's stop preaching and start meddling for a minute. Why do many of us use "doing for others" as our false solution for finding safety? Often, we resist being humbled. Being the "giver" in a relationship can keep us from lots of difficult needs, such as

   our own loneliness
   our inability to ask people for comfort
   our helplessness
   our feelings of being "one down"

Jesus taught that it was more blessed to give than to receive (Acts 20:35). For many of us, it's also easier and less threatening. The only problem, however, is that when giving protects us, it has just turned to selfishness. Then, both the giver and the receiver lose out. Ask God to help you receive *and* give well.

6. Doing "Cosmetic Personality Surgery"

Another futile yet very common approach to finding safe people is making external changes in ourselves that aren't true heart changes. These attempts often give us false hope ("I'm making positive changes") but can disappoint us greatly.

Keith, a friend of mine in school, was exquisitely anxious around people. He wanted friends, but fears of being himself kept him feeling quite out of place. I would watch him squirm at a party and hurt for his awkwardness.

On a suggestion, Keith took a course in social techniques. Not a bad course for certain needs, the class provided ways to get to know people. One of the techniques they taught was to "ask people how they are." The underlying assumption was that people love to talk about themselves, so ask and listen and they'll like you.

A few weeks later, Keith and I went out for dinner. And something unusual happened. Normally, I would take the conversational initiative with him, sensing his uneasiness. But tonight he said, "So, how have you been?"

I was shocked and pleased. And I began to open up and tell him about my struggles. *Wow,* I thought. *Keith's taking a real interest in me.* Perhaps a safe relationship was developing!

I got to the end of some part of my life, and there was a short silence. Then Keith said, "So, how have you been?" for the second time in ten minutes.

Poor Keith. I didn't have the heart to say anything about his gaffe, because he was trying so very hard. But it was obvious that his anxiety was still running at 200 percent, so much that it was drowning out anything I was saying. Fear of intimacy, not an intro line, was what Keith needed help with.

Other examples of cosmetic personality surgery might include:

going to cultural events you have no interest in
participating in sports you don't like
going to churches that are good meeting places, but which
    don't give you anything spiritually
hanging out with people you don't like because they might be
    good referrals for other contacts

This false solution prohibits growth of the real self. The real self is lost somewhere inside, as the false self takes on its own pseudo-life. Remember that God wants to develop the proper working of "each individual part" of his body (Eph. 4:16 NASB). You are one of those individuals. Ask God to help you become the unique person he intended. That person is much more likely to find safety than the pretend one.

7. Doing Without

This false solution is last for a reason. Doing without is the final resting place of many who have tried the first six false solutions. It is where people go who have given up hoping for relationship. It is a place of quiet despair.

When doing the same, the opposite, too much, nothing, for others, and to yourself fall through, you are left looking at yourself, alone, in a mirror. The very isolation of the dilemma is a judgment on you. It judges in several ways, telling you things like:

You aren't meant for safe people.
You don't qualify.
You've been asking for too much.
You can't get it right.
You are too damaged to have relationships.
You aren't spiritual enough.

Typically, people who are trying this last false solution don't make a big fuss about things. They get their lives in order. They bury themselves in work, service, or other worthwhile venues. And they try not to think about what they're doing without.

The disconnected part of the soul isn't a very rude or demanding entity. It tends to die quietly, gradually withering away like a starving infant. After a period of time, you may no longer even be able to feel the pain of isolation. At that point, less pain but more damage is occurring. If you are in this position, part of you is still alive. You're reading this book—even if you're weary, cynical, and with no hope. But you are taking a step.

Because this last false solution is so prevalent and so hurtful, we will spend more time on it in the following chapter, examining why we often choose to isolate ourselves from relationships.

God hurts for your aloneness. He feels what you are going through. And even more, he wants to remove you from these seven deadly false solutions and set you on a new path. As you read the next section, ask God to make known to you "the path of life" (Ps. 16:11). The path to safety is his path, and he wants to walk on it alongside you.

CHAPTER EIGHT

Why Do I Isolate Myself from People?

TED CAME TO see me (John) for depression. A married Christian father, he was a professional man and deeply committed to his faith and family. He'd been depressed for several years, and neither spiritual discipline, faith, jogging, nor vacations had helped.

He entered a group I was leading, which had people working on similar issues. After a little hesitation about talking in a group, he jumped in and got involved in the process.

Ted was caring and empathetic to the pain of other people. He was well-liked by others in the group. But one night, a member confronted him: "Ted, I don't think I know where *you* hurt. So it feels like I don't know you at all."

This sent Ted reeling. He'd figured that "all of him" was in the group, as he really cared for these people. He had not realized that he was that cut off from his own feelings. But the woman was right. "I guess there's a part of me that shut down a long time ago," he said.

What happened from that point on was very hard for Ted, but very important work. He started having memories of himself as a very small boy that he'd never had before. And they weren't fond memories.

He remembered being left alone by his parents for extended periods. Too small to walk, he would cry for a while, hoping that someone would come and pick him up. But no one ever came.

"I think that was the point," Ted told us, "that I gave up on being loved. I can remember now, very early in my life, that it hurt too much to keep wanting love, to keep crying, and to keep reaching out. There was an empty blankness on the other end where a mom was supposed to be. At some point when I got older I remember saying to myself, *I'll stop needing people. And I did.*"

Many of you have tried again and again to connect with safe people, only to find pain and failure. And now you've simply given up. You've stopped the attempt and the search. It's just not worth it anymore. As a client of mine explained, "I really can survive on my own. It's much less messy than taking another risk to be hurt again." I couldn't disagree with her.

This chapter explains the dynamics of withdrawal and isolation. Here, we'll help you understand the most important reasons you might have given up the fight to find the right kinds of friends, churches, and loved ones. And we'll help you see biblical solutions.

A Broken Heart

Ted, in the story above, suffered from a broken heart. For the rest of his life, until he went for help, Ted never again reached out for relational help. He learned to avoid those longings and needs, to stuff them deep inside his heart, and to cope with his broken heart.

Ted's depression was the only thing that saved him. Otherwise, as he put it, "I know myself. I'm absolutely sure I'd have gone on forever, totally out of relationship. That would have been a cakewalk for me." But his broken heart kept sending him the clinical signs that there was a problem. And he finally went to do something about it.

Our hearts aren't all that strong. God has constructed us with certain needs and certain limitations. Our most basic and primary need is to be loved by God and people. We can put that need off, we can meet it in crazy ways, and we can try not to feel it, but it's simply a spiritual reality. Paul illustrated that need well when he wrote, "The eye cannot say to the hand, 'I don't need you!' And the head cannot say to the feet, 'I don't need you!'" (1 Cor. 12:21).

When our need to internalize, or take in, others for sustenance, is thwarted, we are injured. Part of our heart goes hungry. Just as internal organs begin to break down when we don't have enough food, our hearts start to break down when we do not receive love. Enough of this, and we enter the condition the Bible calls brokenheartedness. God has a special tenderness for this difficult condition: "The LORD is close to the brokenhearted and saves those who are crushed in spirit" (Ps. 34:18).

The brokenhearted person has — literally in the Hebrew — a "burst" heart. She has lost the ability to trust, to need, and to reach out for attachment. Many times she has been set up to be connected and receive love from people important to her. And each time something has broken down. Her deprivation is so great that she can no longer function relationally. The relationship breakdown happens in several ways: through abandonment, inconsistent attachment, and attack.

Abandonment

Like Ted, some people are left emotionally by a significant person. This may be a parent, a spouse, or a friend. The important thing is that you have to be attached to be abandoned. That is, you had the person inside you for a period of time, and they mattered to you. Then, for various reasons, the person leaves. This can be physical abandonment, such as a mother leaving the home or dying. And it can be emotional, such as a depressed, overwhelmed, or alcoholic parent or spouse who simply removes the emotional supplies from the person.

Whatever the situation, if the relationship is significant enough to us, we attempt to reach out for the lost person for a while. Then part of us despairs and loses hope, sinking deep inside us as a man sinks into quicksand. We lose our sense of expectation of love, and eventually we lose our sense of need. This is the brokenhearted condition: "I looked for sympathy, but there was none, for comforters, but I found none" (Ps. 69:20). The aching heart simply turns itself off.

Inconsistent Attachment

A second cause of brokenheartedness comes from being loved in an unpredictable manner. You may have someone in your background who was a roller coaster. It was feast or famine for you. And you never knew what to expect. They were close, then either not there or enraged.

Inconsistent connections break the heart in a different way than abandonment. Instead of longing for lost love, the person in relationship with an inconsistent person is always waiting for the other shoe to drop. He thinks, *It's good now, but for how long?* He always worries that the love given will be snatched away. How different inconsistent love is from the love of God, who shines the warm light of his love on us steadily and forever: "My Father, who has given them to me, is greater than all; no one can snatch them out of my Father's hand" (John 10:29).

Attack

We are never more vulnerable than when we need relationship. By its very nature, love means putting yourself out to someone and giving them the opportunity to hurt you. Love doesn't exist outside of risk.

But there are those who deliberately hurt the hurting. You may have someone in your life who criticized or even abused you for having the need for love. Some people, projecting their self-hatred on others, have a deep contempt for the needy. Some are self-centered. Some are sadistic, gaining pleasure in pain: "For he never thought of doing a kindness, but hounded to death the poor and the needy and the *brokenhearted*" (Ps. 109:16, emphasis mine).

If your need for love has been attacked, you probably learned very quickly how to shun relationship and find other ways to pass the time. Like a beaten dog scurries away from a hand that wants to pet it, the broken heart sounds an alarm of danger at any semblance of closeness.

If you qualify as brokenhearted in any or all of these three categories — in your past or in your present — remember that God "heals the brokenhearted and binds up their wounds" (Ps. 147:3). Realize that your isolation isn't really working for you. And begin searching for people who have enough constant, safe love inside to understand how hard this is for you — people that we will describe in part 3. Safe people are out there. You just have to find them.

Self-sufficiency

My three-year-old son, Benny, is now firmly ensconced in the "I can do it!" stage of life. The other day we were getting ready to go out to dinner, and everybody was ready but Benny. He'd gotten all ready except for his pesky Velcro-strapped tennis shoes. They just wouldn't cooperate.

Being the helpful father (actually, the hurried father), I bent down to fasten his shoes for him. He quickly pushed my hands away, protesting, "I'll do it! I'll do it!" And he meant it. So we negotiated. I put him in the car and let him put the shoes on while we were driving to the restaurant. It was win-win.

Now, Benny is in love with autonomy, task mastery, individuation, and a lot of other developmental aspects of his growth. He is working on self-sufficiency, especially in the functional, "doing" parts of life. But Benny's self-sufficiency is a little different in the relational, "loving" areas of life. Instead of task mastery exhilaration ("Look, Ma! No hands!"), he is still dependent on attachment. He needs snuggles, holding, soothing, and comforting. He certainly disagrees a lot more, and he likes to spend more time away from his parents, but the need for connection is still there.

That need for attachment will keep changing over time, and eventually, if things work out, Benny will have enough of us inside him (literally, he'll have "had enough of us"). Then he will get his emotional needs met by peers and finally, by his own family. But he'll continue to grow in his functional self-sufficiency.

People who avoid relationships have problems not with functional self-sufficiency but with relational self-sufficiency. The problem with the relationally self-sufficient person is that he operates in his own relational world. He runs his emotional affairs like a one-man business. His emotional philosophy is the following:

I take care of my problems.
I don't burden others with my problems.
I can handle my problems myself, thank you.
I'm fine, really.
No, really, I'm fine.

What's wrong here? God doesn't create us to be relationally self-sufficient. He loves us to need each other. Our needs teach us about love and keep us humble. True self-sufficiency is a product of the Fall.

If you've got the disease of self-sufficiency, you've probably had it a long time. And you've probably described it in positive terms like *responsible*, *independent*, and *grown-up*. Indeed, self-sufficiency has lots of advantages, because you get to avoid all the uncontrollable problems and risks that needy people can't get away from. Here are a few examples:

> You don't have to experience your incompleteness, which is painful.
> You don't have to go to the trouble of finding people to love you.
> You don't have to show other people the hurting, imperfect parts of yourself.
> You don't have to look anyone in the eye and say, "I need you."
> You don't have to risk asking others to comfort and support you.
> You don't have to humbly receive what they offer, in gratitude.
> *And* you don't have to do it again and again and again.

No wonder giving up self-sufficiency is so difficult. Life seems to have many more problems when your needs start leaking out.

What to do? If your self-sufficiency is driving you away from relationship and into isolation, begin the process of confession. Confession is telling the truth, and the truth is, you need people. The reason people say confession is good for the soul is because it brings unloved parts of our character to places of love.

Find people that understand self-sufficiency. They'll know you can't "feel your need" for them. But they'll help you state your isolation, talk about the reasons you're disconnected, and discuss how hard it is to give up your independence. As you confess this problem to safe people, a wonderful miracle happens: over time, self-sufficiency melts and gives way to need. You are then reconciled not only to God and others, but also to yourself.

Let the love God has provided begin to melt the cold, hard ice of your self-sufficiency.

An Inability to Experience Hunger

Call this problem "spiritual anorexia." You've most likely read about the clinical condition anorexia nervosa, in which the individual starves herself for psychological reasons. The word *anorexia* actually means "no appetite." If you talk to an anorexic about why she's not eating, she'll report, "I'm just not hungry." And she means it. There are several causes for this condition, but it's obviously a dangerous one.

Likewise, in the spiritual and relational arena, some people literally cannot feel their hunger for relationship. They starve themselves when they should be connecting with others, because often they aren't aware of their need. They are numb to their emptiness.

Yet God created within us a hunger, a longing to be known and loved. This hunger functions exactly like physical hunger. It's a signal. It causes discomfort, a warning saying, "Get up and get connected. Your tank's empty." Hunger keeps us aware of our needs, and God responds to that: "God sets the lonely in families" (Ps. 68:6).

Generally, this numbness develops over time as a protective measure. Ted, mentioned at the beginning of the chapter, had this condition. Spiritual anorexia occurs when the heart has been let down, disappointed, or hurt so many times that our "need neurons" simply stop firing. It's as if that part of our character is saying, "Why feel hunger? No one will be there anyway." And so part of us cuts off the sensation of need.

It's easy to tell if you have this condition. Here are some of the classic hallmarks:

I am uncomfortable with people and relaxed when alone.
I don't get "lonely," whatever people mean by that.
I spend time with people out of obligation, or for functional reasons (tennis partner, commuting to work, etc.).
My fantasies of vacation always involve my doing something fun by myself.

Now, God also created us to spend time alone. We need to get away. But spiritual anorexia dulls the senses so much that we can be in real emotional trouble—depressed, ready to act out compulsively, or worse—and the idea that "I might need to call someone" will not even occur to the spiritual anorexic. For them, relationship isn't a hunger—it's an unneeded option.

If this is your condition, God wants to waken a sleeping part of you. He wants you to hunger and thirst for righteous and loving people (Matt. 5:6). Begin now to work on experiencing your need for relationship.

Devaluation

Alison, a woman in my growth group, was hurting over a guy with whom she'd just broken up. It had seemed the right thing to do. The man had lied several times, and he wasn't loving towards her. But Alison still missed him. So she asked for the group's input.

Peter, sitting across from her, almost exploded. "Alison," he said, "This is crazy! He doesn't deserve you! He lied, he hurt you, he'll hurt you again. He isn't worth it!"

Alison thought for a moment and then said, "Peter, you're not letting me grieve."

Wise words from Alison. What in the world did she mean by them?

Simply that we can't let go of anyone until we can feel what is called *ambivalence*—good and bad feelings—toward them. That's what letting go and forgiveness are all about. Alison needed to be able to miss the good parts of her boyfriend, while hating the bad parts that hurt her.

Alison had recognized that in his protective vehemence, Peter was devaluing her old beau. He was seeing the man as less than he was, less than God made him. Why? Because that's how people like Peter deal with loss. *If I think about their bad qualities*, they say to themselves, *it won't hurt and I won't need them so much.*

And that is the essence of this fourth dynamic in choosing no one: devaluation destroys the love that could save us. It protects us from the pain of reaching out. It's the "sour grapes" mentality: "Those grapes I wanted probably weren't any good anyway." Translated, this means, "I really wanted those grapes. Since I can't have them, it hurts inside, and I don't like that sort of pain. Making the grapes bad makes me hurt less."

If you tend toward devaluation, here are some traits you might have:

When I have a loss, I quickly find reasons that the loss didn't matter.

When I lose a relationship, I think of that person's negative qualities to help get me over it.

When people talk about wanting something (new house, to see a movie, a relationship), my mind moves immediately to what's wrong about what they want (house isn't well constructed, movie was razed by critics, that person isn't good for you).

When I anticipate receiving something, I keep from getting excited by devaluing it (it probably won't work, I won't get the promotion, he'd never go out with me).

Devaluation robs us of our excitement, our needs, our wishes, and our desires. It protects us from risk—by keeping us dead inside. You aren't alive if you aren't in need. As a popular song title says, "I Do Not Want What I Do Not Have." That is devaluation: making ourselves not want what we don't have.

Where does devaluation come from? Devaluation is a coping device which we use when love has not worked for us. Reaching out for connection is work. It's risky and humbling enough, even with safe people. But if you've been around unresponsive people for a while, it's more than work. It can be torture.

There are few things more painful than asking for love and finding no one there. Like an exposed nerve ending in your body, your need waits, naked and unprotected, feeling all its hunger. And with no relationship on the other end to soothe, comfort, and care, the pain of reaching out is intolerable.

To compensate for this sort of emotional agony, we devalue what we need. Finding all sorts of creative reasons why we wouldn't want him or her anyway helps us make it another day. Job understood the risks of unrequited love: "For the despairing man there should be kindness from his friend; Lest he forsake the fear of the Almighty" (Job 6:14 NASB). In other words, if my human relationships are devoid of love, I may even turn away from my divine attachment.

What can a devaluer do? Do you make good people bad? Do you avoid taking risks by devaluing? If so, there are several things you can do to help yourself get over that pattern:

1. Realize that you were created to need, and that even God himself experiences longings, as Christ did when he mourned over his unrepentant people: "'O Jerusalem, Jerusalem, you who kill the prophets and stone those sent to you, how often I have longed to gather your children together, as a hen gathers her chicks under her wings, but you were not willing'" (Matt. 23:37). Need is a good part of you.

2. Begin to observe the devaluing things you say and think. Ask friends for feedback on your devaluing. You may be surprised!
3. Observe the patterns. Do you devalue more when you really want something? A friend of mine recently was auditioning for a part in a church play. He loved acting and had an intense desire to be in the program. Yet when he told me about it, he said, "Well, it's just a church play." Often, the intensity of our devaluation is a marker of the intensity of our need.
4. Work on bringing your needs to relationship. Most "devaluers" have tremendously deep fears of being without and impoverished. Find safe people who can help you experience your needs without being hurt.

Perfectionism

Mark is a walking dilemma, one of those people who's hard to figure out. He is an unmarried Christian professional man with no "horrible" problems like drugs, sex, or compulsive addictions. He's intelligent, athletic, and good-looking. He's responsible and loves God.

Mark is forty-five years old. And he has no friends, safe or otherwise. He is very, very alone.

How does that picture come together? On the outside, it doesn't make sense. A guy with Mark's qualities should have a rich, active relational life. But when you understand the power of perfectionism, it makes "perfect" sense. For Mark is a perfectionist and has only recently seen the devastating consequences of this trait.

Sometimes we make jokes about our perfectionism: "I looked in the mirror and got depressed about being three pounds overweight." The genuine article, however, can be much more serious. Perfectionism can be a major cause of depression, destructive behaviors, and divorce.

What is perfectionism? Simply put, it's an inability to tolerate faults. Perfectionists have a phobia about imperfections and blemishes in themselves, in other people, and in the world. They spend enormous amounts of time trying to create a perfect world, running in futility from the realities of sin, age, loss, and cellulite.

The perfectionist tries to live in the land of ideals. He sees life the way "it should be." People should treat each other right. I should be a productive, successful person. Fairness and equality should rule.

Then he sees the huge chasm between the land of ideals and the land of the real. For example, he cannot live up to his expectations of himself. Or he is let down by someone important to him. And he has great difficulty accepting where he lives—the land of the real. So he tries to change his permanent address to ideal-land again.

On a deeper level, the perfectionist lives under the Law. He is in bondage to a demand that says, "If you do it right, you'll be loved." And that is exactly what the Law does say: "For whoever keeps the whole law and yet stumbles at just one point is guilty of breaking all of it" (James 2:10). It's a terrible tightrope to walk, knowing that one slip—just one—brings condemnation and hatred on yourself. While having ideals and goals is good, when our goals become demands—minimum standards—we're being perfectionistic.

There are two ways that perfectionism can cut us off from safe relationships. First, perfectionism disqualifies us from connection. The impossible standard of who I "should" be towers over me like a threatening cloud. I am constantly and acutely reminded of my failings, sins, and weaknesses. I see all of my badness in all of its badness.

And I understand the condemnation of the Law. I feel utterly unloved and alone, knowing my badness cuts me off. At this point the perfectionist begins to develop a grandiose view of his failures, and a minimal view of God's love. He thinks, at some levels, *No one could love the real me. It is too negative, too ugly, too bad.* And he isolates, protecting himself from his deep conviction that anyone who saw the "real" him would turn and walk away from him.

Second, perfectionism disqualifies others from connection. Sometimes the condemning, judging spotlight of the perfectionist gets turned from himself to his relationships. And it is just as stark and unforgiving. He will see others' blemishes and be blinded to any other, lovable parts of them. He will obsess on fixing the other person to make her right, or he will simply leave the relationship.

The perfectionist is often critical of others, though he doesn't mean to be. Often, he is simply projecting his own deep self-hatred on others and attempting to relieve the pressure a little.

Often, the perfectionist feels entitlement—the need to be treated specially, not as another ordinary person. When you are entitled, you may refuse to reach out because the other person doesn't meet your expectations of "specialness."

Here are some things you might do if you have this bent:

You might disqualify a friend before really getting to know her.
You might be enormously hurt and disappointed when someone fails you, and withdraw.
You might have impossible standards for people to meet.
You might become so self-condemning that you avoid connections.
You might have a string of failed friendships behind you and simply give up because the failures hurt so much.

If we're playing "This is Your Life" in this section, there are several things you can do:

1. Understand that you've turned ideals from goals into demands.
2. Begin to study what the Cross actually accomplished: we can be both loved and flawed at the same time.
3. Find out where you learned to be a perfectionist. It could have been a conditional relationship, a perfectionistic parent, or a legalistic religious background.
4. Seek out people to confess your faults to. Note: these must be people who also admit their faults and have no need to judge you.
5. Begin to allow others to both know and love you. Most perfectionists can't do both: they either feel loved and unknown—or known and unloved. Remember that the antidote to perfectionism isn't being good—it's being loved.
6. Give up your sense of entitlement.
7. Begin to do what God does with these issues: take your needs off the Cross—and nail your perfectionism and isolation up there.

Merger Wishes

If this sounds like a familiar term, then you probably read Chapter 6: "Why Do I Choose Unsafe Relationships?" This dynamic also plays an important role in why we choose to isolate ourselves from others.

A merger wish is basically love minus boundaries. When someone else possesses a trait that we don't have, we are inclined to blur our identity with theirs in order to help us feel better about ourselves and to gain access to that trait. Merging also keeps us from feeling alone.

Many people fall in love, get married, develop platonic friendships, and go into business arrangements, all fueled by merger wishes. They will see a creative quality, a loving quality, or an aggressive quality in the other, and do anything to be with that person.

Sometimes the "merger" will feel so excited to be with the "mergee" that she seems intoxicated, swimming in the pool of love with the beloved. Now, in new relationships this is common, and there's nothing wrong with it. That is, as long as you don't make character decisions based on it.

How does this relate to choosing nobody? It does sound strange, because you would think that a merger wish would drive people to "meld" with one person after another. And it does. Some people spend their entire lives trying to fulfill their addictive urge to be totally enmeshed with another person. But there are also times when just the opposite happens.

Vicky picked up the phone and called. When she heard Rick's voice on the other end, she hung up. She ate another bowl of chocolate chip ice cream. Then, her courage bolstered somewhat, she called again. But this time she disconnected before Rick answered. Finally, Vicky hung up even before she finished dialing. She returned to her bowl. It was going to be another "one gallon night."

Now, this scene, familiar to many of us, may look like devaluation. It may look like being unable to need. But it isn't. It was a classic case of "merger-wish-induced" isolation. Here's what was going through Vicky's mind as she struggled with calling her boyfriend:

I want the connection with Rick to be wonderful.
I want us to have no conflicts or misunderstandings.
I want him to understand me, and me him, totally.
I want Rick to comfort me and help me feel better.

But along with those longings, Vicky also had these disturbing thoughts:

What if he's in a bad mood?
What if he doesn't understand me the way I need it?
What if there's a conflict?
What if he tries, and I'm still disappointed in his empathy?
What if it becomes undeniably apparent that Rick and I are two
separate people?

People who struggle with merger wishes are sometimes terrified and discouraged by the realities of separateness. People disagree with us, don't understand us, have to call us back because they're drying their hair. And the "merging" person basically comes to the conclusion: "It's better to be without than to risk the reality of feeling separate. If I'm going to feel abandoned, I don't need the added pain of being with someone."

This is a problem in separateness. To the "merger," separateness doesn't feel like freedom but total abandonment. Separateness becomes the worst kind of isolation to the merger. That's why they frequently try to think up things to say when there's a silence in a conversation: the separateness is too painful. Back to the merge.

If this is a struggle of yours, you may have, like Vicky, given up on relationships. You may have been disappointed too many times and felt abandoned. Here are some action steps to take, to get you back on the road to choosing connections:

1. Realize your trait is probably the result of a relationship in which you were abandoned and made helpless. People who struggle with merger wishes often have been punished for being aggressive and reinforced for being compliant.
2. Begin to make separateness your friend. Distinguish separateness from abandonment, and aloneness from loneliness. Understand how letting others be separate frees you up to make choices yourself.
3. Find people with whom you can practice setting boundaries. Quite often, boundary work helps us love separateness, choices, and our own power to take care of ourselves and do God's work.
4. Be honest with safe people about the merger wish. Unsafe people will move away from you or exploit your needs. Safe people have good boundaries and will stay connected to you, helping you reach out for the love you need. And, as

you are nurtured by separate relationships, you will out-grow the need to constantly "swim in love." Separateness will no longer feel like abandonment.

Passivity

I once stood by and watched a friend's entire life go down the drain. It took several years, but he finally lost everything and every-one he loved.

Kevin was one of the most laid-back guys I'd ever met. Nothing was ever important enough to galvanize him to some kind of action. I always wondered what would happen if you discharged a .38 next to him. My fantasy was that he'd slowly turn his head and murmur, "Sounds like a Smith and Wesson."

Kevin was great to watch sunsets with. I enjoyed taking walks with him and just hanging out. But Kevin, under the guise of being "easygoing," was passive. And it hurt him.

I watched him lose promotion after promotion in his job, because the other guys always had more "fire in the belly." I watched him lose friends, as more active people would get tired of being with him while he just "be-ed."

It was hardest to watch his wife, Lois, and their kids gradually move him out of their hearts. They'd try to provoke him to take some sort of initiative, but he'd just smile and read the paper. Finally, Lois left and took the kids with her. And he didn't put up a fight. Kevin was the nicest guy in the world—but he never took stands, never disagreed, never confronted, and never reached out.

Actually, I did a little more than watch. I'd tell him, "Kevin, I'm concerned that you're going to lose Lois and the kids if you don't make some attempt to be there more with them." And he'd smile and nod, and say, "You know, that's a really good point. I need to think about that." Not surprisingly, nothing would happen.

Kevin is like a lot of people, maybe more severe than most. To be passive is to avoid action, for various reasons. Passive people are patient. They don't mind waiting for things. They believe that "good things happen for those who wait." And they do that better than anyone.

There can be several causes for passivity, such as

a wish to be rescued from their problems by a caring person
a fear of loss if they reach out to someone

a fear of punishment if they take action
a fear of failure
a fear of success

Sometimes passive people spiritualize their condition. They call it "handing over to God." They'll "wait for God" to do things to help them, such as

find them a job
find them a mate
solve relational problems
find them a support group
heal emotional pain

This is an unbiblical view. God never reinforces passivity. He always presents our growth as a partnership with him. He does what only God can do, and we do our job: "work out your salvation with fear and trembling" (Phil. 2:12). To avoid responsibility is never a spiritual act.[1]

Warning: passivity is hazardous to your health. If you're passive, you may find that it's hard to reach out and take initiative in relationships. You may wait by the phone, hoping someone will call. You may wait for someone at work to befriend you. You may wait for a church member to greet and welcome you.

There's nothing wrong with desiring these kinds of encounters. But remember that you'll need to do your part, too. "And if he shrinks back, I will not be pleased with him" (Heb. 10:38).

Don't let life pass you by as you shrink back. Don't let passivity create a mummylike, survival-type existence for you. Find people who want to help you enter the world, encourage you to take action, and support your attempts to regain control over your life and relationships.

Conclusion

Odds are, in these last two chapters, you've seen yourself in a few areas. There are reasons you choose to get into unsafe rela-

---

[1]For more information on this issue, see our book *Twelve "Christian" Beliefs That Can Drive You Crazy*, chapter 4, "I Just Need to Give It to the Lord" (Grand Rapids: Zondervan, 1994).

tionships. There are also reasons you avoid developing relationships at all.

Now that you've understood the problem, it's time to look at the solution. We've stressed over and over that the cure for bad relationships can only be found in developing good relationships with safe people. Therefore, in Part 3, "Safe People," we will help you understand what safe people are, why we need them, where to find them, and most important of all—how to become a safe person yourself. Finally, we will look at some of your less-than-perfect relationships and discuss whether you should repair them or replace them.

PART THREE

Safe People

CHAPTER NINE

What Are Safe People?

I [JOHN] HAVE a fitness fanatic friend named Mark who evangelizes me on the gospel of health whenever he has a chance. He's a lovable guy, but he's the kind who always finds a way to change the conversation to exercise, diet, and vitamins.

We were having breakfast one day, and he began talking about his struggles with his wife, Diane. They were going through a painful period and having lots of conflict. Instead of giving advice, I listened and tried to understand what Mark was going through.

As we talked, he expressed everything from sadness to frustration to anxiety. By the time we finished, however, his face had relaxed, and he could actually smile and joke around.

"You look like you're feeling better," I said.

"Absolutely, I'm more encouraged," Mark said. "Wheat toast, fruit, and herbal tea make me a new man!" Then he looked at me and grinned sheepishly. "Uh, and it might have helped to have someone to talk to," he admitted.

Though Mark wasn't sure about that fact, I am. What happened at breakfast is that I acted as a safe person for Mark to confide in. Just as surely as we were taking in our breakfast to sustain us physically, so we were talking to sustain ourselves emotionally. We were enjoying the great benefits of a safe relationship.

What Is a Safe Relationship?

We like to think of a safe relationship as one that does three things:

1. Draws us closer to God.
2. Draws us closer to others.
3. Helps us become the real person God created us to be.

The Bible refers to these three areas of spiritual growth. We fulfill the greatest commandment, to love God (Matt. 22:37–38). We keep the second commandment, to love each other (Matt. 22:39). And we grow into the particular person that God created us to be, accomplishing the tasks he has designed for us (Eph. 2:10).

When we asked people to describe a "safe person" to us, they gave us these descriptions:

A person who accepts me just like I am.
A person who loves me no matter how I am being or what I do.
A person whose influence develops my ability to love and be responsible.
Someone who creates love and good works within me.
Someone who gives me an opportunity to grow.
Someone who increases love within me.
Someone I can be myself around.
Someone who allows me to be on the outside what I am on the inside.
Someone who helps me to deny myself for others and God.
Someone who allows me to become the me that God intended.
Someone who helps me become the me God sees in me.
Someone whose life touches mine and leaves me better for it.
Someone who touches my life and draws me closer to who God created me to be.
Someone who helps me be like Christ.
Someone who helps me to love others more.

We would all want people in our lives that help us in these ways. But the problem is, how do we recognize them? What do they look like?

We all struggle on different sides of the "safe relationship" issue. Some do not even think we need relationships with other people. They think the Lord is enough and that you should only trust in him. Others think that they must depend only on themselves. Still others believe that the Bible teaches the value of relationships, but then they find themselves in hurtful relationships over and over again. They pick hurtful friends, spouses, churches, work partners, spiritual leaders, and dating relationships. They seem to not have the ability to find and like safe people. Having a seemingly astounding talent for finding people that will ultimately hurt them, they repeat patterns over and over again, and then become discouraged about relationships in general.

So, for us to begin to utilize safe relationships, we need to first understand what a safe person is and why we need that kind of safety.

The best example of a safe person is found in Jesus. In him were found the three qualities of a safe person: dwelling, grace, and truth. As John wrote: "The Word became flesh and lived for awhile among us. We have seen his glory, the glory of the one and only Son, who came from the Father, full of grace and truth" (John 1:14).

Dwelling

Dwelling refers to someone's ability to connect with us. Strong's Greek dictionary tells us that the Greek word used here means to "encamp" or "reside." It says that the origins of the word have to do with the human body as the place where the spirit resides. What all of this means is that safe relationships are an aspect of the *incarnational* qualities of Jesus, for Jesus became present as a man, in the flesh. They are able to "dwell with us in the flesh." They are able to connect in a way that we know that they are present with us.

Many marriages begin to experience this lack of safety, as one of the partners complain of things like "They just aren't with me. I can't feel them in the way that I used to." Or "they seem so far away."

Grace

The second safe quality that Jesus exemplifies is grace. Grace is "unmerited favor." It means that someone is on our side, that they are "for us." Grace implies unconditional love and acceptance with no condemnation (Rom. 8:1; Eph. 4:32). Relationships in which people do not accept us without shame and condemnation are ultimately hurtful and do not produce growth. They require us to be different than we are in order to be accepted, and we are unable to use love that we must earn.

Grace does the opposite. It says that you are accepted just like you are and that you will not be shamed or incur wrath for whatever you are experiencing.

Truth

The third quality that Jesus embodied for us was truth. Truth implies many things, but in relationships it implies honesty, being real with one another, and living out the truth of God. Many people think that safe relationships are relationships that just give grace without confrontation, but as we will see later, these relationships are ultimately destructive as well.

We need people in our life who will be honest with us, telling us where we are wrong and where we need to change. We need friends that walk according to the truth and live out the principles of God with us. This does not mean that they are not accepting, but it means that in their acceptance of us that they are honest about our faults without condemning us. "Brothers, if someone is caught in a sin, you who are spiritual should restore him gently. But watch yourself, or you also may be tempted" (Gal. 6:1).

True safe relationships are ones where we can speak the truth to one another, confronting each other as needed. Grace and the absence of condemnation allow us to do this with less fear than would occur in a condemning relationship.

In the rest of this book, we will be examining different aspects of dwelling, grace, and truth. The calling of the Bible is that we need to be the kind of people to each other that Jesus is with us, people who dwell with each other in grace and truth.

CHAPTER TEN

Why Do We Need Safe People?

M ANY HAVE FELT the pangs of the psalmist who wrote: "It is better to take refuge in the LORD than to trust in man" (Ps. 118:8).

I remember a pastor we worked with who was very depressed and on the verge of giving up the ministry. When we began unraveling his depression, it became clear that he was a deeply isolated person. He had many friends, but he did not allow anyone to get close to him. As we explored this emotional isolation, we found that when he was a young boy, his brothers had hurt him very deeply. Being smaller and younger, they made fun of him in groups, and they also betrayed him individually.

One day, when he had been humiliated by them, he said to himself, "I will never trust anyone again." And, true to his word, he lived out that promise. The problem was that it took its toll on him through the years. Having hundreds that he ministered to and was around all the time did not fill the void inside that the wall had created.

Jesus showed the way to break down that wall. Again and again, he and his followers taught that good human relationships were one of the primary ways that God changes our lives and heals us (1 Peter 4:10).

The Church

There is great misunderstanding today about the role of the body of Christ. When people are hurting they do not think of turning to the body of Christ as God's agent to answer their prayers, to heal them, and to help them develop. We often want to pray and

147

have God miraculously show up himself and make things different. We pray about depression or some character trait and want Jesus to appear in a white robe, touch us, and make us mature.

The incredible thing about this wish is that Jesus *has* appeared! He did appear on earth "in the flesh" as John 1 told us earlier. And in this appearance, he modeled for us the love we should have for one another, and he told us to become a body, or church, where we can know and experience his presence through union with him and with each other. It is in church that we fully know and experience his touch on earth today.

The problem is that we think he has abandoned us and that we can only truly touch him through mystical union. Although direct mystical spiritual relationship with God is certainly primary and important, the Bible does not separate our relationship with God and our relationship with people in his body. In fact it says that if we do not have good, loving relationships with people, we do not know him either (1 John 4:20). *What many Christians do not understand is that relating to each other is a spiritual activity.*

We too often think of our spiritual life as just being with God, but he tells us that spirituality is a life of love both with him and with each other (Matt. 22:37–40). We need to include in our evaluation of our spiritual lives the question, "How am I doing with other people? How are my relationships going?" Often we get caught up in thinking that service is the only indicator that we are growing spiritually, when in truth our human relationships are always one of the key indicators of our spiritual life.

Jesus came down to earth not only to save us but also to show us how to love God and others. The church often emphasizes our relationship with God and de-emphasizes our relationships with other people. But the Bible says that both are important; we really cannot have one without the other.

The Bible teaches very clearly that we need others in order to grow into the people that God wants us to be. In this section, we will look at some of the specific reasons why we need other people in our growth process.

Fuel

Jane was running down. As the weeks went on she became more and more depressed and tired. She did not feel the energy to "get up and go." She had lost all her motivation, and basically she wanted to stay at home most of the time.

She came into the hospital because the depression was getting worse. Her internist felt that her chronic fatigue might be emotional. As we began to learn more about Jane and how she felt inside, we found that he was right.

Jane had been hurt a lot in her early relationships. As a result, when she would get into situations that were conflictual or where someone was not approving of her, she would begin to feel as if she were worthless and unlovable. As that feeling increased, she would withdraw from just about everyone, including her family. In this withdrawal, she would gradually become more and more tired and less motivated.

It was difficult for her to understand, but her tiredness was being caused by her disconnection and isolation from other people. As she isolated herself emotionally, she would not have the "fuel" from others that we need. "And not holding fast to the Head, from whom the entire body, being *supplied* and held together by the joints and ligaments, grows with a growth which is from God" (Col. 2:19 NASB, emphasis mine). We actually are supplied with what we need from others in the body of Christ. Good old-fashioned support is basic fuel to be able to face and deal with life as it presents us with trials and discouragements.

Comfort

When Paul was depressed and discouraged, God comforted him by sending him a friend. "But God, who comforts the depressed, comforted us by the coming of Titus" (2 Cor. 7:6 NASB). Many times the Bible tells us to comfort others with our presence, help, and words. Romans 12:15 tells us to "mourn with those who mourn." People who are grieving will tell you that a combination of God's presence and the support of other people gave them the comfort they needed. We are not self-sufficient. We need to get things from others, and comfort is one thing that we are not made to give ourselves.

"I thought I would never get over the death of my husband," Penelope said. "I would lie in bed at night unable to sleep, and think that my chest was going to tear in half because of the pain. The only way that I made it through was because of my friends who would sit with me while I despaired. It was not what they said that helped; it was the fact that they were there."

For Strength in Setting Boundaries

One of our greatest needs for emotional and spiritual health is to have healthy boundaries. We need to have the ability to say no to evil, and sometimes this evil comes from hurtful people. Sadly, we sometimes don't have the strength to stand up to it.

Mary tried to be loving to everyone in her life, but whenever a relationship required something other than "love," she was at a loss. If a relationship required her to be strong and stand up to someone in the way that Matthew 18:15 tells us to do, by confronting someone who sins against us, Mary was unable to do it. She would fold when the other person became angry or controlling.

As the years went on, she was continually feeling overrun and controlled by her husband. He became more and more abusive to her and the children and even started drinking heavily. When she would tell her friends, they would all tell her to give him a strong ultimatum. He needed to get help, or move out. Every time she would try, he would get angry, and she would fold.

Finally she got into a support group for spouses of problem drinkers. The members of the group began to make a stand with her, modeling for her how to deal with him and offering the support she needed when the conflicts came. As she got the necessary support she needed from the group, she knew that she would have some people to go to when things got tough. She did not have to fold because she knew her friends would be there for her. They were doing what the Bible tells us to do when it says, "Therefore, strengthen the hands that are weak and the knees that are feeble, and make straight paths for your feet, so that the limb which is lame may not be put out of joint, but rather be healed" (Heb. 12:12–13 NASB). We need others to give us the strength and discipline to set and keep boundaries in some very tough situations.

We have seen many peoples' lives and families change dramatically when one family member finally got enough support from a good group to make a stand against evil. They never would have been able to do it by themselves, as years of trying had proven. But with good supportive safe relationships, they found the strength they needed to make changes.

Foundation for Aggression

Often we think of aggression as something negative. But aggression can be good, helping us achieve our purpose in life. Passive people do not know how to use their God-given aggression to go out and attack life and accomplish the goals that God has put before them.

Patrick was such a person. Raised by a very passive father and a domineering mother, he had the familiar "passive man" syndrome. Many of his dreams went unfulfilled, and his responsibilities went unmet. Both he and his wife were frustrated. Because he had never had the modeling from strong men that he needed to internalize a sense of his own strength, he would just procrastinate and fold.

When Patrick finally got into a good, safe support group with some strong men, he got the modeling his father never gave him: modeling to go out and be strong and face life. We cannot internalize abilities we have never seen; these men gave him the models that he needed to identify with to become the strong man that his wife needed him to be. Good relationships in our new family, the family of God, can give us the things that our original families did not provide for us.

Encouragement and Support

"Fighting the good fight" is discouraging, and we often need direct encouragement from God and his Word (Rom. 15:4; Phil. 2:1). But the Bible also emphatically says that we need to be encouraged by each other: "Tychicus, the dear brother and faithful servant in the Lord, will tell you everything, so that you also may know how I am and what I am doing. I am sending him to you for this very purpose, that you may know how we are, and that he may encourage you" (Eph. 6:21–22).

We often think of the apostle Paul as a spiritual giant who was somehow so spiritual that he didn't need anything from others. But he writes in many places that the encouragement and love of others kept him going through difficult times. We are never so "spiritual" that we do not need the encouragement that God provides through other people. That is how he designed it: "Two are better than one, because they have a good return for their work: If one falls down, his friend can help him up. But pity the man who falls and has no one to help him up! Also, if two lie down together, they will keep warm. But how can one keep warm alone? Though one may be overpowered, two can defend themselves. A cord of three strands is not quickly broken" (Eccl. 4:9–12).

Modeling

Many people come from families that do not teach and model God's ways (Deut. 6:7; Prov. 22:6). Such people are unequipped to do the things that life demands that we do in order to be happy and successful. We do not have anything that was not first given to us (1 Cor. 4:7). All of us are lacking in certain areas of life where we have not received the modeling we needed. Like we saw above, this could be in the area of strength or boundaries. But there are many others: compassion, empathy, love, marriage, career development, fun, talents and skills, relationship skills, forgiveness, sex-role development, and on and on.

We all came from a dysfunctional family: the family of Adam— the human race. In that family, we all came to adulthood underdeveloped. God looked upon us and said, "You guys need more than help. You have got to start over." We cannot just pick up where we are; we must be "born again" and become like children. We need to learn to live all over again in his family with him as our Father.

God gives us the body of Christ to parent us and other people to teach and mentor us. Paul emphasized this in many ways and would encourage people to follow his own modeling and to do the same for others (1 Cor. 4:16–17; Titus 2:3–8). He called Timothy his child in the Lord and modeled to him the way to live. Later Timothy was able to model Christian living for others as well. In this way generational health is passed on in the family of God the way that he intended the children of Israel to do it.

Healing

Emotional healing has many aspects to it, but one of the major pieces to healing any emotional disorder is grief. We need to grieve painful events, painful losses, love that will never be realized, dreams that have been crushed, and many other hurts that life inflicts upon us. All of these ultimately are healed through a grief process. This is why Jesus said, "Blessed are they who mourn, for they will be comforted" (Matt. 5:4). He also said that in order to grow, we have to be able to let go, to "lose" our old lives, and this is a grieving process of severe loss (Matt. 16:25).

We cannot lose and grieve what we need to grieve without something new to attach to. This is why so many people never get over the emotional hurts from childhood, or forever seek the love and approval from a parent who was unable to give it: they have never been able to grieve because of the lack of something new to replace what they need to grieve.

Grieving takes a new relationship. We must have God and others to connect to in order to let go of what we have lost. As Paul told the Corinthians, if they would connect to him, they could let go of their other "affections," or emotional ties that were "restraining them": "Our mouth has spoken freely to you, O Corinthians, our heart is opened wide. You are not restrained by us, but you are restrained in your own affections. Now in a like exchange—I speak as to children—open wide to us also" (2 Cor. 6:11–13 NASB). Many people do not get healed because they never "open wide" to others in the body of Christ, thus gaining the support and new ground needed to stand on to grieve what they need to let go of. Healing without grief does not happen, and grief without support and new love does not happen either.

Confrontation and Discipline

One day I (Henry) had a conflict with Joe, a member of our staff, about an acquisition bid, and I got very angry with him. He had also gotten very angry at me, and the meeting had ended on a terrible note. In our meeting later that night I had hoped that our other team members would see how unreasonable he had been and come to my aid to confront him about a certain pattern in his life that had caused us a lot of grief.

The meeting started with my wanting to face the issue and confront Joe. I talked for a while, and then Joe talked for a while. I was ready for the other team members to jump in and support me. But that is not what happened. They all confronted me on the way that *I* had responded to *him*. They went on to say that they had had the same experience with me that Joe had talked about. One of them years before!

I couldn't believe it. Here I was hurt by him, and they were confronting me! Together, they all made me aware of times that I had not listened to their feelings, but was quick with an argument. I was surprised. I thought I was the injured party, but the truth was that I needed to change a pattern of relating. I began to see how I did the same thing in other relationships. It was a helpful, but painful, thing for me to learn about myself.

This incident illustrated a very important biblical principle of the value of "safe people" in our lives: for confrontation and discipline. My team members loved me enough to confront me and tell me where I needed to change. I was not aware of my need to change. If it had not been for them, I probably still wouldn't know it. I needed them, and I did not even know it!

This is an important point. The areas that we usually most need to change, we are unaware of; know, but resist owning; or we know and openly rebel against. All three of these stances demand intervention from the outside. We need our brothers and sisters to make us aware of our behavior, confront our denial, and take a stand against our rebellion. If we remain in some hurtful or sinful pattern, a true friend will come to our aid to save us from ourselves.

"Brethren, even if a man is caught in any trespass, you who are spiritual, restore such a one in a spirit of gentleness; looking to yourself, lest you too be tempted" (Gal. 6:1 NASB). The Bible is clear about the necessity of our letting each other know about the ways in which we need to change, and it emphasizes the nature of those relationships. They must be humble, honest, gentle. That is the essence of "grace and truth."

If we fail to hear such a confrontation, the Bible does not tell us to just ignore the sin. It tells our brothers and sisters to get even tougher with us, coming together as a group to make a stand against our hurtful patterns:

"And if your brother sins, go and reprove him in private; if he listens to you, you have won your brother. But if he does not listen to you, take one or two more with you, so that *by the mouth of two or three witnesses every fact may be confirmed.* And if he refuses to listen to them, tell it to the church; and if he refuses to listen even to the church, let him be to you as a Gentile and a tax-gatherer. Truly

I say to you, whatever you shall bind on earth shall be bound in heaven; and whatever you loose on earth shall be loosed in heaven" (Matt. 18:15–18, emphasis mine).

This process of "intervention" can be very painful and conflictual, but it is so important for us to save each other from ultimate destruction. I have seen some pretty terrible situations turned around because a group of believers had enough love to get together and confront a friend who needed it.

Discipline and confrontation are two of the best gifts our "new family" of safe relationships in the body of Christ can give to us. We need to make sure that we are looking for those kinds of safe relationships, and we also need to make sure that we are not what the Bible calls a fool, someone who will not heed the discipline of others (Prov. 12:5; 15:5; 17:10). If we are, we are headed for destruction and many more "unsafe relationships."

Good Deeds

I just received a letter from two high-school kids who took their first missions trip. Both from Christian families, they were always "good kids." But they wrote to tell me that their lives had been changed in an even deeper way because they had gone with other believers and seen service in action and what it can do. It was being around other Christians that had pushed them into a new dimension of life that is better than any: service to others.

The Bible tells us that we do not just think of "doing good" on our own. We need to be stimulated by each other to do good things. Our relationships help us to be encouraged to lives of service. "And let us consider how we may spur one another on toward love and good deeds. Let us not give up meeting together, as some are in the habit of doing, but let us encourage one another—and all the more as you see the Day approaching" (Heb. 10:24–25).

We need to be around others who help us to grow and become the people who God made us to be.

Rooting and Grounding

Dennis and I had planned to play golf on a Saturday, and I was looking forward to it. My phone rang late on Friday evening.

"Sorry to call so late," Dennis said, "but I had to call and tell you that I won't be able to play golf in the morning."

"Why not?" I said. "I was looking forward to it."

"I can't play because I'm broke," he said.

"No, really, why can't you play?" I asked. Dennis was a wealthy man.

"No, I'm serious. I'm broke."

"Yeah, sure. And I'm Jack Nicklaus. Really, why can't you play?"

"Somebody has embezzled everything I have, and I'm really in trouble. I have been investing with a money manager for about a year, and it looks like he has taken all my liquid cash. It's bad because I had a lot of money liquid to close some really big deals on significant pieces of land. I am going to lose everything that I have put up. He has done this to about twenty of us, and I got chosen by the investors group to make the trip to Germany tomorrow to try to stop the deposits."

I couldn't believe what I was hearing. Here was one of the smartest businessmen I knew, and he had been cleaned out by some thief.

"Here's what I want you to do," said Dennis. "Can you meet me for lunch next Thursday at the club?"

"Sure," I said. "I want to hear all about it."

He hung up, and I began to feel really sorry for him. He was quite a guy and one of my closest friends. On top of his money struggles, his wife had left him only a short time before and had taken the children with her. That is about all a man has: his wife, children, and work! My heart bled for my friend.

Next Thursday came, and I looked forward to hearing his story. I was surprised when I showed up and found that he had invited others as well. They were all seated around a table.

"Guys," he said, "I'm busted. It looks like I have lost everything. It is really bleak. But here's what I need from you. If each of you will sign up for a day a week to have lunch with me, if I know that I will see one of you every day, I can make my comeback. If I know that I have your support, then I can do it."

He wanted to know that he could lean on his friends while he tried to put his life back together. In about a year and a half, he had done it. He had made a financial and spiritual comeback.

What was Dennis's secret? Was it his business sense and ability to weather stress? Sure. But he had something else also, the most important element in a significant and successful life. He knew that he had to be connected somewhere, grounded somewhere, since everything in his life had disappeared. All of the structures that had given him a sense of what day-to-day life was about had suddenly gone. But he did know that he still had God and his friends to depend on and that, in those relationships, he would be able to find the grounding and stability that he was going to need to put it all back together. It was this sort of grounding that Jesus prayed for in John 17:11, 22: "Holy Father, protect them by the power of your name—the name you gave me—so that *they may be one* as we are one. I have given them the glory that you gave me, that *they may be one* as we are one" (emphasis mine). He knew that they would have to be a safe unit for each other first before they could do the work that he had for them.

The Bible refers to the body of Christ as being "knitted together" in love (Col. 2:2 NASB), and this helps give us the support that we need in order to grow and go through the trials of life. We need to be grounded in the body of Christ in a way that is unified to give us strength. Unity is the first thing that Jesus prayed for for the disciples, knowing that it was the most important. When we build our lives in this way, obeying his word, the winds and the rains can come, and we will be able to weather the storms (Matt. 7:24–25).

Love

In relationships we learn to love. We receive love, and this teaches us how to love. We love "because he first loved us" (1 John 4:19). Loving people are loving because they have been loved, and they have followed that example. This is what Jesus taught us, to love others as he loved us (John 13:34).

As we have also seen, one of the important ways that he loves us now is through the body of other believers. They are the instruments of his grace (1 Peter 4:10). As we place ourselves into good relationships that are loving and receive and respond to that love, we learn how God wants us to love others, and we can go and do likewise.

It is also in our relationships that we learn the ways in which we fail to love correctly. It is only as we relate intimately to others in the body of Christ that we find out how unloving we can actually be. They tell us, we apologize, receive forgiveness, and then try to do better. Through this process of failure, forgiveness, and growth we find out the areas and ways we need to change, and God is then able to change us.

I would have never grown in the way that I needed to if I had not been involved closely enough with people that I would get tested. If we never have close relationships, we can be under the delusion that we really are loving. It is only in the testing ground of real love, not concepts, that we get stretched and tested.

We have talked about what safety really is: dwelling, grace, and truth. And we all need this safety from other people. God designed us for safe people, and in the context of his family of safe people, we can grow into the image of his Son, who was and is the ultimate Safe Person.

CHAPTER ELEVEN

Where Are the Safe People?

I got an emergency call, and the office relayed to me that I had a suicidal client. I called Theresa on the phone. She was distraught.

"Tell me what happened," I said.

"It's not going to work," Theresa replied, sobbing.

"What isn't going to work?"

"Telling other people about my problems," she said. "I went to my fellowship group tonight and told them about the depression and the problems with Joey, and they really came down on me for being depressed and for all the other stuff that has been going on."

"What did they say?"

"Well, they said that I shouldn't feel that way and that if I was still having all those problems then I probably wasn't walking with the Lord. I don't know what to do anymore. I've tried all this 'safe relationship' stuff, sharing and all that, and now it doesn't work."

"What would you say if I told you that you still haven't found safe relationships?" I asked.

"What do you mean?" Theresa asked. "They are all Christians and in my church."

"Well, Christian doesn't automatically mean 'safe,' " I told her. "Safe is defined by helpful. It doesn't sound like tonight was too helpful."

"Well, how do you know a helpful relationship?" she asked.

"That's a good question," I said. "Let's talk about that."

I empathized with Theresa. She had discovered a real truth: the church is not a perfectly safe place. That sounds like it cannot be true, for if anywhere should be safe, the church should be. Every fiber in our being rejects the idea that the one place we think *ought* to be safe — the house of God — isn't.

The church is not a totally safe place, and it does not consist of only safe people. As much as we would like for it to be totally safe, the truth is that the church has to be seen the way God describes it. We must, if we are going to have a biblical view of relationships and people, and live the way that God wants us to live, see the church as he describes it. Our faith must be able to square with the reality of life as we find it *and* with the reality that the Bible describes to us. Let's look at those two realities.

Reality as People Find It

Theresa was echoing the experience of many people. Anyone who has been in the church for very long has been hurt by people in the church. For in the body of Christ, we find some harsh realities: judgment, pride, self-centeredness, manipulation, abandonment, abuse, control, perfectionism, domination, and every kind of relational sin known to humankind. The walls of the church do not make it safe from sin. In fact, the church by definition is composed of sinners.

To further complicate matters, church by its very nature as a family of God activates our most primitive and dependent longings because we want a perfect family. God designed the church to be our second family, and often we take into the church the same longing for security and love that we take into our families of origin. And for some, as in their original family, the wish is not only disappointed — it can be crushed altogether. What are we to do with that reality?

The one difference is that, as adults entering into the family of God, we have choices about who we are going to trust and get close to. David said in Psalm 101:6 that we can pick the "ones who will minister to [us]." But we are not by nature so discerning. We come into the church feeling and wishing, "Take care of me. I need you. I shouldn't have to first figure out who is safe and who is not. You should be good and trustworthy." We feel the longing of Romans 8 that says that we long for and groan for our adoption. We want things to be right. And then they are not.

On the other hand, many of us have felt that the body of Christ has nurtured, loved, and taught us in ways that have radically healed us. Through the acceptance and love of other believers our character has changed, and we have slowly let go of the things that shackle us.

We also hear others testify to that reality. They were destroyed by their families, or the world, and they were saved and healed in their church. Someone — or a group — in the church reached out to them, and their lives were radically changed.

I (Henry) can testify to this. I had dreamed and planned my whole life to play professional golf, from the age of six until I was recruited by a nationally ranked college to play varsity golf. I was beginning to compete on higher and higher levels and doing quite well. I thought my dreams were being realized.

Then catastrophe hit. A tendon problem in my left hand snatched my budding career right out from under me. I could no longer even hold onto a golf club, and there was no cure. I was lost and devastated. The path that I had diligently worked towards for fifteen years, day and night, had hit a dead end. At the same time, I encountered some other significant losses in my life. Things were falling apart. I got seriously depressed.

At first I tried to work my way out of it. I had always been a "don't ever give up" kind of person, especially in sports. I thought I could lick this problem in the same way, through sheer hard work and willpower. But I got more and more depressed, and nothing was filling the hole inside of me. The depression and lostness continued to build until I decided to drop out of everything to try to sort things out.

I first reached out to God, telling him that I did not even know if he existed, but that if he would show me that he did, I would do what he told me to do. After all, my way wasn't working.

Less than an hour after I prayed that prayer in a little chapel at Southern Methodist University, my phone rang. A friend I hadn't talked to in quite some time told me that he and some others were starting a Bible study and that for some strange reason, he thought that he would invite me to come. I told him I would, not quite believing what had just happened.

To make a long story short, the leader of that Bible study and his wife invited me to come live with them for a semester while I sorted things out. Their gift of themselves to me forever changed my life. Their love and teaching touched some very deep parts of me as they led me to the reality of a relationship with God. He had found me, and through the love and acceptance of his body, I was being healed.

So the church can be a healing place, a place where lives are transformed and where powerful love and healing can take place. The body of Christ is still God's instrument for our healing and restoration (1 Peter 4:10; Eph. 4:16). So, the question arises and rings in our needy hearts: Is the church safe, or is it dangerous? The answer is, "It is both." Sometimes we are fortunate to find good relationships, and other times we run into disaster.

Reality as the Bible Describes It

The sad thing is that our ideals for the church do not reflect biblical reality, either. We think that the Bible promises a church where we find only safe people. But the Bible says that the church is full of wolves as well as sheep. In the church, we will find both tremendous healing and potentially tremendous hurt. And if we are going to find healing and minimize hurt, we need to make sure that we see the church as God describes it to us. We need to operate according to biblical reality instead of our fantasized wishes, for biblical reality is the one that will fit the experience we find in the real world.

In describing the reality of the kingdom of God, Jesus told a story:

> The kingdom of heaven is like a man who sowed good seed in his field. But while everyone was sleeping, his enemy came and sowed weeds among the wheat, and went away. When the wheat sprouted and formed heads, then the weeds also appeared.
>
> The owner's servants came to him and said, "Sir, didn't you sow good seed in your field? Where then did the weeds come from?"
>
> " An enemy did this," he replied.
>
> The servants asked him, "Do you want us to go and pull them up?"
>
> " No," he answered, "because while you are pulling the weeds, you may root up the wheat with them. *Let both grow together until the harvest*. At that time I will tell the harvesters: First collect the

weeds and tie them in bundles to be burned, then gather the
wheat and bring it into my barn."

(MATT. 13:24 – 30, emphasis mine)

As this story shows, God allows unsafe people to be in the
church. They are wolves in sheep's clothing, and they are dangerous. While they may seem religious, they may not even be true
believers. While they do many things in his name, they are not his
sheep (Matt. 7:22 – 23).

Another reality is that even with true believers, we get a mixed
bag as well. Listen to the parable of the sower:

> When anyone hears the word of the kingdom, and does not
> understand it, the evil one comes and snatches away what has
> been sown in his heart. This is the one on whom seed was sown
> beside the road.
>
> And the one on whom seed was sown on the rocky places, this
> is the man who hears the word, and immediately receives it with
> joy; yet he has no firm root in himself, but is only temporary,
> and when affliction or persecution arises because of the word,
> immediately he falls away.
>
> And the one on whom seed was sown among the thorns, this
> is the man who hears the word, and the worry of the world,
> and the deceitfulness of riches choke the word, and it becomes
> unfruitful.
>
> And the one on whom seed was sown on the good ground, this
> is the man who hears the word and understands it; who indeed
> bears fruit, and brings forth, some a hundredfold, some sixty,
> and some thirty.

(MATT. 13:19 – 23 NASB)

Within the church some people are never really born again; the
kingdom never even takes hold in them. Some people are joyful in
the faith, but they do not have the reality of the life of God within
them. Both of these groups can be very destructive.

But it is in the third group where we can get really confused. The
seed has taken hold, they are in the faith, but they are so self-centered
and caught up in temporal concerns that they are not producing loving fruit in their relationships. And this kind of well-intentioned, but
not growing, person can be very hurtful as well.

Finally, Jesus describes the fruitful person. This person,
although not perfect, is involved in the process of growth with
God. Love, confession, humility, truth, and grace are present and

increasing. And that kind of person is the one that brings about healing in other people's lives.

Wisdom and Character

Our experience and the Bible affirm the same thing. The church is full of safe people, unsafe people, and hurtful lingerers. There is no perfect family short of heaven. But there is also no absolute hell full of demons either. And the Bible's clear message is that we need to be discerning. We need to make informed choices, and we need to be careful. But we also need to avoid becoming pessimistic and learn to recognize the goodness that abounds within the family of God (Matt. 25:34 – 40). If we become skeptics and give in to our fears of bad outcomes, God says that we will lose the little that we have.

So, the long and the short of it is that we have to work to find safe people, using our wisdom, discernment, and character. We gain wisdom and discernment through knowledge and experience. But if our own character problems get in the way of using our knowledge and experience we will make poor choices, as we have discussed in earlier chapters. We need to make sure that we are facing the weaknesses inside and dealing with them, becoming people of character who can choose other people of character, with a knowledge of what they look like. As we get the log out of our own eye first, we will be able to see clearly.

Some Options

Within the body of Christ, God has gifted people to heal each other (1 Peter 4:10; Eph. 4:16). We have found these people in a variety of settings and structures, from informal to formal. Here are some of them.

Safe Churches

One place where one can find safe people is in churches that have a safe character as a group. Many churches have good orthodox doctrine, but they are not bodies where relationship is really preached and community is formed. Safe churches, however, have the following qualities:

- Grace is preached from the pulpit and is the foundation for how people are to be treated.
- Truth is preached without compromise, but also without a spirit of law and judgment.
- The church leaders are aware of their own weaknesses and need to grow and are open about their hurt, pain, failings, and humanity. Instead of "having it all together" and being insulated from confrontation and change, they are in a process of healing and opening up to their own safe people for support and accountability.
- The church uses small groups to touch people's lives, and sermons focus on community in the body of Christ as well as doctrine.
- The culture is one of forgiven sinners, not self-righteous religious Pharisees.
- The church, instead of being a self-contained unit and thinking it has all the answers, is networked into the community, availing itself of input from other sources such as churches, professionals, and organizations.
- The teaching has a relational emphasis as well as a vertical one. Relationship between people is seen as part of spirituality as well as relationship to God.
- The teaching sees brokenness, struggle, and inability as normal parts of the sanctification process.
- There are opportunities to serve others through a variety of ministries.

Churches have personalities and cultures, and it is possible to find churches that fit the above characteristics.

Restorative Friendships

We value friendship. We believe that friendship is one of the most powerful tools that God uses to change and heal character. In relationships with others we are healed, our character is changed, and sanctification happens. We know several people who have developed a support system of restorative friendships that have been of enormous help.

I was talking to a woman just yesterday who had significant struggles with her son because of her inability to set limits. Louise was desperately afraid of boundaries and felt like she was being mean if she put her foot down. With a history of hurtful, perfectionistic friendships, she had suffered much because of her lack of ability to stand up to others.

Louise's mother had always played the martyr with her, making her feel guilty about having limits in their relationship, and not accepting her wanting to have a life of her own. In addition, her mother had been very critical, and Louise always felt as if she were failing in her friendships with other women.

Things began to change when she and another woman with similar problems committed to each other to meet twice a week and go through some materials on setting boundaries. They promised to pray, support, and confront one another. Eight months later, things really began to change for Louise. With her friend's support and prayer, she was getting stronger and finding that her limits and boundaries could be loved as much as her performance and achievement. The friendship had begun to heal her.

Friends give us what we need in the areas of acceptance, support, discipline, modeling, and a host of other relational ingredients that produce change. But in picking good friendships that produce growth, several qualities are important:

- acceptance and grace
- mutual struggles, although they do not have to be the same ones
- loving confrontation
- both parties need other support systems as well to avoid the same kind of toxic dependency on each other that led to the problems
- familiarity with the growth process where both parties have "entered in" and have some knowledge of the process so as to avoid the blind leading the blind
- mutual interest and chemistry, a genuine liking
- an absence of "one-up and one-down" dynamics
- both parties in a relationship with God
- honesty and reality instead of "over spiritualizing"
- an absence of controlling behavior

Friendships of this kind are an absolute must for our spiritual growth.

Support Groups

Groups are an extremely powerful tool for spiritual and emotional growth. A dynamic occurs in a group that is absent in one-on-one relationships. Members realize the universality of pain and suffering, and they are not as tempted to condemn themselves.

Group support can be extremely powerful, as we can more easily devalue the support of one person. A group forms an army to fight against our self-loathing and destructive patterns. While we, or one other person, may not be able to stand up to our character problems, a group is stronger (Eccl. 4:12).

Support groups come in many styles, from therapy groups to twelve-step groups, to prayer groups, to groups that form around a particular issue, such as grief or sexual abuse. These groups can be especially helpful because they exist for the expressed purpose of helping hurting people. Many times people will say that they know they need some support, but they are afraid to trust. Group members expect a person to have problems if they have joined the group, and they can accept each member and help with the inability to trust. If you have a problem with trust, this can be a lot better than just going out and trying to find or meet people who are worthy of trust.

One caution needs to be mentioned, however. Groups are powerful and need leadership by people who know what they are doing. They need to know the issues that will arise and how to deal with them. That is why groups have trained leaders, or leaders who have experience in the growth process. We generally discourage informal groups of hurting people who get together with no trained or experienced leader. These groups can re-create all the problems that someone is there to get help with. Unless you are far along in the process, try to find groups that are structured, have an expressed purpose, and have experienced leadership.

Individual Therapy

Sometimes people are so hurt and have so much to deal with that they need specialized one-on-one attention. Individual therapy is a powerful, proven method of dealing with deep issues and developmental impasses. Research has shown that it is the best method for dealing with some deeper kinds of personality issues and specialized problems.

In choosing a therapist, remember that you are a consumer and have a right to know that you are getting good care. Do not pick a therapist haphazardly. Check out her credentials first, and make sure that you check around with people who are familiar with her work. Pastors are a good referral resource. Ask your pastor who has a good reputation for dealing with your particular problem. A good reputation in the community is an important guide to an experienced and helpful therapist. By their fruits you shall know them.

Be Careful and Go for It

There are many good people out there. To find them, make sure that you use discernment, wisdom, and information, and trust your experience with people. If someone is destructive or producing bad fruit in your life, be careful. Keep looking, praying, and seeking until you find safe people — people who will give you all the benefits that God has planned for you.

CHAPTER TWELVE

Learning How to Be Safe

I F YOU'VE LIVED in a neighborhood where there are no leash laws, you've probably seen a medium-sized dog chasing down a large car. I used to watch my dog Little Bit do this a lot when I was growing up, and I'd always wonder to myself, *What's Little Bit going to do with the car if she does catch it? Take it home? Bury it? Eat it?* I never got an answer, because she never succeeded.

You may have that same question as you've worked through the issues of identifying safe people in your life: *When I find one, what do I do with him now? Look at him? Go to a movie? Ride off into the sunset?* Remember, we're an action-oriented culture. Many of us are quite unfamiliar with the dynamics of closeness.

The good news is that we can take action to become more intimate. These actions lead us into deeper connections with God's people, which then sustain us for life and growth. That's the issue of this chapter: How to be safe once you've found safety. There are several major tasks and opportunities ahead of you when you make the connection. Let's take a look at them:

Learn to Ask for Help

Stacy was anxious. She'd been in my counseling group for a while, working on problems in relationships. A married mother of two, Stacy had spent a large part of her life taking care of people. These included her husband, her kids, and her emotionally dependent mother, who always needed Stacy to "be strong."

Stacy had begun to see how she was attracted to needy people and avoided being with giving people. She was always surrounded by charities, crisis cases, and ministries who knew she'd make herself available. But she was starting to understand how terrified she was of allowing people who could give to her to get inside her.

Stacy told me, "I realize I need people, and I don't ask for anything. What do I do?"

I said, "The people in this group care about you, Stacy. They've grown to know you and love you. Several people here today would probably like to offer you something. But you'll need to let them know."

Stacy was bemused. "Let them know what?" she asked.

"They need to know that you're empty inside, that you have weaknesses and insecurities, and that you want them to tell you they care about you even when you're weak. That'll do for starters," I answered.

Stacy smiled a little. "Sounds good. Only one thing . . . you've already told the group I need to connect with them. Can that count for my saying it?"

After the group laughter died down, Stacy faced her friends. For the first time in her life, she asked people simply to let her know they cared for her. The group responded warmly, surprising her a little. She'd expected more critical comments. But Stacy was now on her way in "doing safety."

The first step is the hardest. Stacy was only half-joking about having me ask the group for her, instead of her asking herself. It isn't easy to ask for help, and it's risky. Yet it's absolutely the first key in using our safe people to help nourish and mature us.

God places a high premium in the value of asking directly for help. Forms of the word *ask* appear almost 800 times in the Bible, many of them an invitation from God for us to ask for things:

- "If you believe, you will receive whatever you ask for in prayer." (Matt. 21:22)
- "You do not have, because you do not ask." (James 4:2)
- "And receive from him anything we ask, because we obey his commands and do what pleases him." (1 John 3:22)

Not only are we to ask God for what we need in prayer, but also other people: Paul wrote his friend Philemon, "Confident of your obedience, I write to you, knowing that you will do even more than I ask" (Philem. 21). Asking is human and divine, because God created us to ask.

Why is learning to ask for love so important? Here are a few of the reasons asking is helpful for us:

1. When we ask, we develop humility.

To request help or support from another destroys any illusions of self-sufficiency we might harbor. Asking helps us remember that we are incomplete, that we are needy, and that we are to seek outside of ourselves to take in what we need. This creates the position of humility in us, which opens us up not only to others, but to God: "God opposes the proud but gives grace to the humble" (1 Peter 5:5).

2. When we ask, we are owning our needs.

Asking for love, comfort, or understanding is a transaction between two people. You are saying to the other: "I have a need. It's not your problem. It's not your responsibility. You don't have to respond. But I'd like something from you." This frees the other person to connect with you freely, and without obligation. When we own that our needs are our responsibility, we allow others to love us because they truly have something to offer. In other words, asking is a far cry from demanding. When we demand love, we destroy it.

3. When we ask, we are taking initiative.

Asking is the ultimate "Passivity-Buster." It helps us out of the trap of wishing and hoping someone will somehow sense our pain intuitively and come to our rescue. This also means that asking keeps us much more in control of our lives. We aren't dependent on the clairvoyance of our friends (what a relief to them!).

4. When we ask, we are developing a grateful character.

God cherishes a grateful heart. He knows that gratitude will produce love in his people. Those who have been helped will help others. Those who have been loved and forgiven little, love little (Luke 7:47).

5. Asking increases the odds that we'll get something.

Though it sounds too obvious to say, it's important. How many times have you neglected reaching out to someone who is now absent from your life? Askers really do tend to get more out of their relationships.

What do I ask for? This is important, because many of us confuse function with relationship here. In other words, we're not talking about borrowing a cup of sugar from your neighbor, or getting a ride to the airport. Asking for functional reasons is fine, but it will not help you develop relationships. In fact, it's easy to avoid relationships by asking only for functional things.

Men tend to have a problem here. We'll sometimes form relationships built on functional neediness. Sometimes this type of connection is called "foxhole buddies," where there's a truly deep affection between two men who have depended on each other through tough times. Yet they may have trouble connecting emotionally.

Learn to ask your safe people for the very things you found them for: a relational connection. Learn how to ask for your emotional tummy to be filled just like you'd ask for breakfast for your physical body. Ask someone to be with you spiritually and emotionally, the same way that Jesus asked his closest friends in his darkest hour: "'My soul is overwhelmed with sorrow to the point of death,' he said to them. 'Stay here and keep watch'" (Mark 14:34). Here are some ideas:

I don't ask well, but I'd like to start connecting with you.
I am in a spiritual and emotional place in my life that I'd like to begin making attachments, and I'd like that with you.
I need you.
You're important to me, and I'd like to spend time learning how to be close.
If you're interested, I'd like to deepen our relationship.

Sound difficult? It is. But asking for help will enable you to internalize your safe people in places of your heart that are darkened, alone, and cut off. Take the first step. Ask.

Learn to Need

In the summer of 1969, a British-born New York neurologist named Oliver Sacks began working in a Bronx mental hospital. He dealt with the patients in a ward named the "Garden." It was given that name because the staff believed all they could do for this peculiar set of patients was to feed and water them.

These patients were victims of the great "sleeping sickness" epidemic of the 1920s. Some were completely paralyzed now, and some simply had bizarre physical behavior. For three decades, these people had simply existed as human vegetables. They were thought to be unthinking, almost brain-dead.

Sacks began studying this group and made an astounding discovery. The "Garden" patients were alive and aware! They were suffering from severe Parkinson's disease, rendering their muscles immovable. But the people within were thinking, feeling, observing individuals who were forced to mutely watch friends and loved ones talk about them as if they were objects—some for nearly thirty years.

Sacks found that administering massive doses of L-dopa, designed to treat Parkinson's, helped these patients regain muscle control. They began moving about and talking. Their sense of wonder at being able to be involved in their world was profound.

Then, tragically, the effects of the L-dopa began to wear off. The treatment, Sacks found, was only temporary. And the reborn again became the unborn. Slowly, they returned to the living tombs inside their bodies.

In 1972, Sacks wrote a book about his discoveries which is now a medical classic, titled *Awakenings*. Then, in 1990, it was the basis of a major film. His work has deeply affected the thinking of many medical and philosophical minds.

Sacks' experiences paint a vivid picture of the emotional state of many individuals. Like the patients in the Bronx "Garden," those of us who have been emotionally detached may also have lost our ability to connect to the outside world. Our needs and hungers are lost somewhere inside, buried alive, with no ties to our "real" life. Life boils down to a sometimes meaningful series of thoughts and actions. A genuine sense of rich connection to others, however, is absent. Our needs sleep within us.

This may be true for you. Your needs for relationship may have been buried. They may be so far underground that you've despaired of ever finding them again. If so, this second task, "learning to need," is vital for you.

This issue relates to the problem mentioned in Chapter 8, "The Inability to Experience Hunger." You may have been hurt, deprived, or disconnected from relationship for so long that the need simply died, leaving you with no experience of "wanting" connection. You know you need people. But you just can't make yourself "want" people.

And yet God created you to long for attachment, to desire to matter to someone and to "hunger and thirst" for relationship. He made you that way, so that you could know when to seek comfort and connect. Just like your car's gas gauge, your needs tell you when you're on "empty."

You can regain your experience of neediness. You had it once: almost all babies are born with the God-given desire to be protected, connected, and comforted. And God is in the business of redeeming that which is lost, including disenfranchised parts of our soul.

1. Confess your inability to need.

Tell the truth to your safe relationships about how hard it is to rely on others, depend on others, and actually want others close. Let them know that needing them is not a skill, but a goal for you. This lets your friends know that you truly need to need. As they draw closer to you, instead of shrinking back, you slowly learn to trust again. What is occurring is that the internal need begins to respond to the warmth, constancy, and safety of your relationships.

2. Don't fake it.

You might be tempted to pretend you're closer and needier than you feel, hoping you can generate the feelings. This isn't helpful. It distracts your safe people from your real condition and discourages the lost part of you from being known. This will probably take some time, but safe people understand that and have time.

3. Keep your boundaries.

Pay attention to your need for separateness. You might be tempted to become a "hugger" when that activity makes your skin crawl. Or you might think you should spend extended time with people who leave you resentful and overwhelmed with doing "people stuff." This also creates more distance inside. Let people know when you've had enough connecting time, and don't push it too hard. This helps you feel much safer internally, and more ready to take risks, knowing you won't be swallowed up in relationship.

4. Confess the need that you can't experience.

Let people know what you are asking for, even though they know you can't feel it yet. This lets them know you and respond to your real state. Here are some examples:

I need my relationship with you.
I need to know I matter to you.
I need to know my imperfections don't push you away from me.
I need to know that within your own resources, you aren't going
   to leave me.
I need to know you understand.
I need to know you love me.

Bear in mind, you may not be able to feel these truths. That doesn't mean they're less true. And you are integrating as much of yourself as you can into the relationships. This paves the way for the rest of yourself.

5. Pay attention to what evokes your hunger.

Generally, after a certain amount of working on this with safe people, some event will allow the need to emerge a bit. It may be an especially empathic statement from someone. Or they may identify your pain with theirs. Or it could be that they didn't come down critically on you when you brought up a problem.

And something new happens inside. You may find yourself feeling loved a little. Your eyes may mist up. You may feel warm inside. And you might find yourself feeling closer to your friend, and looking forward to being with him again. The need is awakening!

Whenever you sense that you've responded internally to a person, trace down what it is about what they said or did, and how that relates to their character. Tell them what it is about them that you're drawn to, and how it helps you. Tell them you want more of that!

Like a child who finds a favorite stuffed animal, the need within will begin responding more and more to your safe person.

Work Through Resistances

Tom, a Christian businessman who's a good friend of mine, looked around at the faces in his living room. Most were people he'd known for several years at various levels. Tom and his wife, Arlene, had invited them all to their home to discuss a different kind of home Bible study group which they wanted to form. He began talking.

"For a while now," Tom said, "I've felt a need for a group which would add another goal to understanding the Bible. In addition to learning content, doctrine, and application, I want to learn about bonding. I've realized that I avoid connection. I've done it well for many years." He looked over at Arlene, who smiled knowingly.

He continued. "I've asked you people over to be part of a group in which we learn to be vulnerable, open, and honest. And in which we learn how to depend on and trust each other." The group seemed to lean forward in positive anticipation. *This has promise,* their postures seemed to say.

"There's a glitch in this idea, though. And I want to warn you about it," Tom went on. "I don't want to do this. I don't want to open up to you. I don't want to bring you my inner feelings. I have no emotional interest in telling you my hurts. And I really don't want you to open up to me.

"This will be really, really difficult for me. I'd much rather do an information-based study, and hide behind that. It's much more my style. But I've realized that emotional connections are very important for my growth. No, more than important. I won't survive if I don't learn how to make attachments.

"I'm gonna come to this group kicking and screaming. I'll fight it and resent it. But I promise that I'll attend every meeting, and I'll try my best. So what do you think?"

You could have heard a pin drop in the living room. The others didn't quite know what to think. And guess what happened? They decided not to form a group! Tom's honest appraisal of what he needed, and his resistance to that, weren't what they were looking for. In fact, it took a few months and an invitation to a different bunch of people before Tom got the group that he wanted . . . or didn't want.

In his unusual "invitation," Tom was doing something very, very helpful. He was normalizing something for himself and his friends that very much needs normalizing. Tom was normalizing resistance.

What is resistance? Resistance is our tendency to avoid growth. It's our drive to keep the spiritual and emotional status quo. It's our inclination to move away from God's provisions for our growth: "For what I want to do I do not do, but what I hate I do" (Rom. 7:15). And we all have it.

Resistance is actually the thread which ties together chapters 6, 7, and 8. Many of the dynamics which drive us to choose unsafe people and no people are resistances. From needs to rescue to repetition, we're loaded with ways to keep our hearts from encountering loving, supportive people. As crazy as it sounds, we often build entire lifestyles around avoiding those who would help fill us up.

We hope you're more aware of your own opposition to attachment, after having exposed yourself to the principles in this book. You may become more informed about your bias toward critical folks, your passivity, or your detachment. This isn't bad news. It's good news. Now there's something to fix!

Beware of the attitude that you have no impediments to intimacy. That's the unsafest position of all. "Let him who thinks he stands take heed lest he fall" (1 Cor. 10:12 NASB).

Don't fall into the trap experienced by the overeager son in Jesus' story of two brothers and their father employer (Matt. 21:28–32). When Dad asked the son to go to work, "He answered, 'I will, sir,' but he did not go" (v. 30). The son didn't own his resentment of working for Dad. He lost out, and you will too. Accept the reality of your resistances.

How do I deal with them? We've listed how-to's for several of the important resistances in chapters 6, 7, and 8. But here's a bird's-eye view of how to approach resistances:

1. Identify your resistances.

Forewarned is forearmed. The more aware you are of your specific resistances to love, the more power you have over them. Denial is your worst enemy here. With the feedback of friends, make a list of the ways you shrink from safe people, and become a student of these dynamics. They are a "road map" to understanding yourself and your real needs.

2. Bring them into relationship.

My friend Tom is a good model here. He didn't throw resistances into the Bible study as an aside. He made them a focal point of the relationship. It takes humility to ask people to help you work through perfectionism, guilt, or merger wishes. But safe people are the last to throw stones. They've got too much experience with their own issues. You'll find warmth and patience with your resistances. What's more, you'll find that your resistances will begin to melt as you connect.

3. Meet the needs underlying the resistances.

Remember that these oppositions are designed to protect you from hurt. They're obsolete guardians of your soul, like Adam and Eve's fig leaves. And when the true spiritual needs underlying them have been met, they lose their power. The fight is largely over. Actively seek the connections, the truth, the forgiveness, and the equality with others.

4. Do the opposite of what the resistances tell you.

If you're in need, your internal opposition may tell you to do some destructive things, like

Go only to God with this.
Handle it yourself.
Ignore your need—you're feeling sorry for yourself.
Realize it's your moral failure.
Suck it up. Don't be weak.
Find someone to criticize you.
Find someone to caretake.

Rebel! Rebel against the unbiblical authority of the resistances! They'll tell you to find critical, irresponsible, or abandoning people—or to not seek at all. Instead, seek out loving, responsible, and faithful people.

Use the two words the Jews adopted after the Holocaust of World War II: *Never again. I'll never again—at least, as much as is in my power—give in to the abuse to which my resistances have led me.* Take a stand by going against these sorts of impulses.

Invite the Truth About Yourself

I (John) once witnessed a five-year-old girl with a lisp tell a 160-pound teenaged boy, "Rodney, you really hurt me when you thaid I was thtupid." And Rodney had to sit there and accept Janie's words. It was a powerful scene, watching someone so small and helpless confronting someone so large and strong.

The setting was a child and adolescent day treatment center I worked in during my clinical internship. At the center, kids of all ages were treated from 8:00–5:00, Monday through Friday, for depression, conduct disorders, and anxiety problems.

One of the most important times occurred at the last hour of each day, just before parents picked up their kids. It was called "Crosstalk," and during this hour, each child, no matter how old or how severe her condition, was free, along with staff members, to give observations to her peers about their behavior or attitude that day.

Sometimes a kid would praise another for his good work: "I liked it that you played with me today and didn't stay in a corner." Sometimes, the statements were quite specific: "You yelled and scared me three times today. I didn't like it." And, at times, they were quite moving: "You talked nice to me when I was crying today. My heart wanted to sit on your lap."

"Crosstalk" was the great equalizer. No one could "despise your youth" (1 Tim. 4:12 NKJV). And during the months I worked there, I noticed it worked. Kids paid attention to kids' feedback, often more than they listened to the staff. They could trust the truthfulness of one of their own, and they used the feedback to make changes in themselves.

One of the most valuable things you can do with your safe people, ranking up there with asking for help, needing, and melting resistance, is simply to invite the truth about yourself. We have so many blind spots and areas where we aren't aware of our self-destructiveness. The psalmist's invitation to God echoes the same issue: "Search me, O God, and know my heart; test me and know my anxious thoughts. See if there is any offensive way in me, and lead me in the way everlasting" (Ps. 139:23–24). God often uses people to answer that prayer.

We're a lot like children here. Many of us are untrained, inexperienced, and unskilled in knowing how we affect people—except perhaps in untruthful ways (example: "You ruined my life when you didn't visit me last Christmas" is an impossible crime—that would not ruin a person's life—though the person saying it may not think so). So, like kids, we need lots of help learning the issues of life: about love, limits, goodness, and badness.

There are lots of ways to implement this step. You can ask for feedback in a hundred different ways. I think, however, that the important realities can be summarized in two questions. If you will regularly ask these two questions to your safe people, and use the data, your life will flourish. Here they are:

1. What do I do that pushes you away from me?
2. What do I do that draws you toward me?

I can't think of many more difficult words to say to a person, nor more helpful. When you ask these questions, you're saying several important things to your safe people. You're telling them

I value how you feel about me.
I want you to be a very important part of my life.
I respect what you observe in me.
I don't want to hurt you or our relationship.
I trust you with my most vulnerable parts.

What might you receive? Many of us are terrified at the prospect of hearing feedback from others. You may have heard many hurtful or untrue things about yourself from a critical person. Or you may feel that you're a sham, and that others are waiting to pounce on you and expose you to the world.

Safe people just aren't wired like that. Your safe person wants you to know the truth for two reasons. First, the truth increases love. People who are free to be honest are free to love each other. This is because the fear of loss of attachment is gone, and "there is no fear in love" (1 John 4:18). And second, the truth is always your friend. Understanding how we turn people off can go a long way in increasing the quality of our relationships and work lives. This is part of what the truth setting us free is all about (John 8:32).

You'll hear insights, perceptions, emotions, and observations you may have never expected. When people feel truly free to tell the truth, they tend to be quite honest but also quite loving. Remember, your safe person has heard you take the initiative to ask for the truth. There exists no concrete wall of denial to break through. Safe people don't need to use a grenade when a whisper or two will suffice.

You may find out the following truths:

how people feel when you withdraw from them
how much they miss you when you detach
how they would like for you to be more open about your losses
how it hurts them when you don't respect their boundaries
how your imperfections draw them closer
how much your own journey is helping them connect with God
    and others

These are profound and important realities. They are really the sum and substance of life itself, because life's substance is relationship. Value and cherish these truths from your safe people.

Generally speaking, the more rigorous you are with your own self-examination, the better it goes for you. And the converse is true: the more you minimize your failings, the more your safe people have to work in sharing the truth with you. Get real, get honest, and get working on yourself. Which would you rather hear from those who know you best: "Don't be so hard on yourself" or "Wake up, turkey, smell the coffee, and get out of denial!"?

Enter into Forgiveness

Recently, I developed one of those nagging Jiminy Cricket-type reminders that involved an old friend of mine named Ken, whom I knew long before I was married. I kept remembering an event between us that had occurred a long time ago.

I'd hurt him deeply by not being there for him at a bad time in his life—a time when I'd assured him I would be there. I'd neglected our friendship. There was no excuse for my actions. I had offered none, though I was truly sorry and told him that. We talked briefly about it, and that was about it. He hadn't said much about it at the time, but I knew I'd wounded him.

Ken and I had stayed friends over the years after that occasion, and he'd never brought up the subject again. We both got married, had kids, and got busy with our lives. We tried to stay in contact and keep up with each other.

But that Jiminy Cricket voice in my head wouldn't go away, so I figured perhaps I needed to pay attention to it. I have to use discernment with remorseful feelings. Sometimes it's my conscience, sometimes it's God, and sometimes it's a bad pizza I had last night. But I felt I should act on this one.

I called Ken late one night and told him, "For some reason, I've been feeling pretty remorseful for hurting you badly several years ago. And I didn't know if perhaps I needed to ask your forgiveness for that. Where are you on that issue?"

Ken thought a few seconds and said, "Go back to bed. I forgave you then. I knew you were sorry you hurt me. And frankly, I'm much more interested in the rest of our relationship than I am that event. I'm healed from it, and I would have told you if I wasn't."

I went back to bed. And before I drifted off, I told myself, *No more anchovies on my pizza.*

I really don't know what caused the feelings. It could have been my own lack of forgiveness being projected onto Ken. But whatever the reason, here's the point of that story: safe people lead us into lives of forgiveness. One of the greatest benefits you'll find in your safe settings is a deepening understanding of failure and what to do with it. And the answer to that is always forgiveness.

Safe people are a very forgiving people, as we discovered in chapter 7. They have given up on the idealistic demand that they, or anyone else, will be perfect in this life. They know that they continually need divine and human "debt-cancellations." And they expect failure and disappointment from those they love. It's normal in their universe, something to be accustomed to.

They are familiar with the losses and sins of this world, in the same way that Jesus handles loss as "a man of sorrows, and familiar with suffering" (Isa. 53:3). They don't fight it or become indignant or bitter. They know that's just the way a post-Fall, pre-eternity world is. They know that loving is much more important than holding onto the past, as long as the past has been worked through and resolved. They also know how much you need to be familiar with forgiveness.

Learn to be "two-sided" in forgiveness. Use your time with your safe people to learn the two skills of forgiveness:

1. Learn to receive forgiveness.

When we are forgiven in our relationships, we truly know what it is to be "home." Being forgiven for our sins, weaknesses, imperfections, and badnesses means reconciliation. It means that someone else knows and doesn't condemn us.

Receiving forgiveness allows us to integrate judged and condemned parts of ourselves. As we experience someone outside who accepts us as we are, we begin to accept the realities of who we are also. In other words, the parts of our soul stop fighting and trying to kill each other. They start working together, as the gears mesh in a finely tuned machine.

Here are the skills of receiving forgiveness:

Learn to apologize.
Learn to feel empathy for the pain you cause others, rather than guilt.
Learn to admit your faults without rationalizing or making excuses.
Learn to ask, "Will you forgive me for hurting you?"
Learn to take in forgiveness without attempting to make up for your fault, or to pay for your trespass.
Learn to accept the love that knows we are frail, and loves us still.

2. Learn to give forgiveness.

Forgiven people become forgiving people. When your safe people look you in the eye, knowing how you've let them down, and say, "Go back to sleep," the relief, love, and gratitude are immense. You become an evangelist for forgiveness.

The good news about giving forgiveness is that it's not really about the person who hurt you. Forgiveness does free the perpetrator, even though he may be unrepentant, in denial, or dead. But at a deeper level, the person whom forgiveness frees is yourself.

When we use our safe people to learn how to cancel emotional debts, we can become free of the past. Free of the bondage of hurtful memories and experiences. Free of the need for the perpetrator to apologize before we can get on with our lives. And free to love people who are different and more caring than the perpetrator.

When Jesus warned us that "if you do not forgive men their sins, your Father will not forgive your sins" (Matt. 6:15), he wasn't teaching about salvation as much as a spiritual reality of our lives. If we hold on to the hurts of others, awaiting justice, we are less able to take in the freedom of our own forgiveness. Forgiveness is a two-way street. We need both skills.

Here's some things to do with your safe people that will help you in this vital character issue:

> Confess the hurts you've caused others.
> Confess the hurts you've received from them.
> Use the relationships to feel your negative emotions about the injury, such as hurt, sadness, anger, and shame.
> Take in the character elements from your safe people that you needed from those who hurt you. Remember, if you outgrow your need for someone, they lose power to hurt you.
> Process your wish for revenge and instant justice.
> Learn to grieve those wishes and accept the realities.

Your safe people will stand with you through this difficult but highly significant growth process. You may need to trade off with them. When you need to let go of someone or something, they can be strong. When it's their turn, perhaps you can be the anchor.

Give Something Back

My church called me (John) recently to ask if I'd help out in the Sunday school class for two-year-olds. They were shorthanded and needed volunteers. I said yes and showed up that morning.

It was chaos. Temporary space problems had dictated that we had three classrooms of toddlers in one room for that day. And, with all those kids with an attention span of microseconds, we volunteers stayed busy. We played trucks, dolls, read stories, sang, taught Bible lessons, wrestled, changed diapers, and dried tears. Even the seasoned regular workers were exhausted.

The only other man there was, like me, a called-in parent. I asked Brian what he was doing there. He said, "This class does a lot for me. It gives my daughter Brittany a spiritual foundation. It lets me and my wife go to church and receive something, away from Brittany. I know I can trust the people. And my daughter is making friends. I try to get in here and help out whenever they need me. I'm grateful for all they do."

Brian "gets it." He's been given to, and he gladly gives back. That's what this last section is about.

So far, we've laid out the five emotional and spiritual character growth tasks that safe relationships were made for. They are some of the tasks set out in eternity for us to accomplish, as we were "created in Christ Jesus to do good works, which God prepared in advance for us to do" (Eph. 2:10). They build us up, mature and repair us, and most importantly, help reestablish God's image in us. But there's more to life than being helped.

When we receive all that goodness inside us, gratitude takes over. And, just like when we're forgiven, we feel a responsibility to give to others what we've taken in. This is also a spiritual task. And also one with which you'll want to involve your safe people.

Now, restrain the urge to anxiously try to figure out what in the world you can give. It's pretty simple, really. We are limited to giving what we have received, and no more. Remember the widow's mite. There will be needs you can't meet in your safe people, and places they need to go spiritually where you haven't yet set foot. God has someone else ready to help them.

What return can I make? Here are some principles to guide you as you put shoes on your gratitude. And, by the way, if you don't feel grateful, that's something to investigate. It may be because this process has not been going on long enough, and, like a newborn baby, you're still in a major "receiving" stage (1 Peter 2:2). Or it may be because you haven't allowed the love in. Or it may be because you're devaluing it in some way. Make that an issue to explore.

1. Understand what you've gained.

Spiritual and emotional dynamics can be articulated. They're not simply a mystical or emotional experience with no meaning. You may have learned about trust with your safe people. Or that your needs are okay. Or how to be honest. Or when you withdraw. Put words onto these. You'll be surprised, and you'll be better prepared to know what you're giving: "Let the redeemed of the LORD say so" (Ps. 107:2 NASB).

2. Learn your friends' "need signals."

As you become more closely knit to others, you'll pick up cues of their needs. They may become quiet or busy. They may become overwhelmed or experience distressing emotions. Learn to cue in on their emotional presence. Ask yourself, *Is he here with me,* or *Is she somewhere else?*

3. Ask to help.

Safe people want to be in touch with their spiritual status and needs. Simply say, "You've meant a lot to me. Help me know what you need, and what part I can play with my own resources." That is an invitation to a safe person to give you some good information.

4. Be there.

Resist the temptation to solely "love by doing." It might be natural to baby-sit your friends' kids for them, or help out with Saturday chores (though these are much appreciated). In addition, learn to listen to their pain and losses. Get to know what hurts them deeply, and tell them you care about them. Let them depend on you for support. Accept their weaknesses and failings. Become "Jesus in the flesh" for them, for that is how we all are to function as his representative "the church, which is his body, the fullness of him who fills everything in every way" (Eph. 1:22–23).

5. Tell the truth.

Your safe people will also have their own blind spots. Tell them when they are hurting you, themselves, or others. Confront in humility, from one blind spot to another. Don't be parental. But tell them what will help them stay away from harm.

6. Go into the world.

Finally, get out of your "safety zone." Find opportunities to help the lonely, the oppressed, and the less fortunate. Find those who have absolutely nothing to offer you in return. And become a safe person for them. I hear over and over again of people who have received safety then found ways to help others, such as

non-Christians
the poor
minorities
single-parent families
substance abusing people in recovery
those with emotional struggles
AIDS victims
mission organizations
the neighbor next door

You don't have to be a minister or counselor to help others. You can be a significant part of the journey for another person who may have no clue that her issues require a safe person. Receive it, and give it, over and over again.

Conclusion

To become a safe person, you need to practice these six steps over and over again: ask for help, learn to need, work through resistances, invite the truth about yourself, enter into forgiveness, and give something back. These six steps will keep all of us plenty busy for a long, long time. But this is work that has meaning and purpose. It is work that will reap wonderful spiritual and emotional fruit for us and others.

Our final chapter in *Safe People* deals with a thorny question: How do you know whether to repair or replace a relationship that's presently unsafe?

CHAPTER THIRTEEN

Should I Repair or Replace?

W E HAVE HAD a recurring experience over the years as we have taught this material. Many people, finally understanding that we are to discern safe people from unsafe people, then use that knowledge to legitimize blaming others and leaving significant relationships. In fact, they will often even thank us for giving them justification for leaving a relationship or their marriage.

This is upsetting to us, for not only is it a distortion of what we teach, but it is fundamentally unbiblical. The chief theme of the entire Bible is reconciliation of unsafe relationships. This means that no relationship can be left without a struggle to negotiate and resolve problems, even the worst sins known to man. This is a far cry from the easy out that says "When I found that this person was unsafe, I left him."

In this chapter we will find that God did not do that in his own unsafe relationships. He didn't move away from them. He moved toward the relationship and became a facilitator of healing. Let's learn from his personal example.

When God created humankind, he had a long-lasting love relationship in mind. His ideal was for people to stay in an unbroken relationship with him forever. He wanted humankind to eat from all the trees of the Garden, with all of the enjoyment of life and fellowship with him. And he wanted the relationship to last forever, for he gave humans the tree of life—sustaining, eternal life. It was for keeps.

But things did not work out this way. People turned toward self-centeredness and away from God and his ways. And God was faced with the same dilemma that we are faced with in our relationships in a fallen world: Do I keep them, or do I move on?

As we have discovered in life, relationships go awry. They do not live up to the expectations and the wishes that we have for them in their inception. We cry the same cry that God did when his people strayed: "You have hurt me!" (see Ezek. 6:9). We find ourselves torn between feelings of hurt, revenge, forgiveness, compassion, and grief that we even entered into the relationship at all.

What are we to do? When are we to try to reconcile and work things out, and when are we to count the relationship as a loss and move on? When we are thinking about this question, it is helpful to think of how God handled the problem of difficult relationships. Looking at him as our model, we find that God (1) starts from a loved position, (2) acts righteously, (3) uses the community to transform us, (4) accepts reality and forgives us, (5) gives change a chance, and (6) is long-suffering.

Now, let's apply those six steps to our own difficult relationships.

1. Start from a loved position.

When God was planning what to do with his relationship to us, he was already loved. Within the Trinity, God is in an eternal love relationship. For example, in John 17:24 Jesus says that the Father had always loved him, even before the foundation of the world. God did not need us, and that is an important principle for us to remember in establishing and working out our relationships. *If we need any one person in order to survive, we will not be able to resolve the relationship.* Our dependency keeps us from being ourselves and doing the right thing. In order to work out a difficult relationship, we need to be secure in our other relationships. Our support system needs to be intact.

Debbie discovered this truth in her dealings with her "difficult" husband. An "enabler," she would help him to remain in his destructive patterns by covering for his anger and irresponsibility. When he was moody, for example, she would try to appease him instead of confronting his fits of anger and sullenness. When the children showed signs of breaking under his critical spirit and wrathful responses, she worked even harder to make sure that he was always happy. To cover for his irresponsibility, Debbie took on more work. But this did not "cure his self-esteem," as she wished. Instead, her enabling behavior shielded him from the natural consequences of his behavior and allowed him to avoid adulthood.

Debbie's friends encouraged her to take a stand with her husband, but every time she was about to try, she would chicken out and go back to her old behaviors.

Finally, Debbie joined a support group for "enablers." Instead of trying to hide the fact that the marriage was in serious trouble, she began to open up to others about her pain. *As she became connected to the other members in the group, she found that she was not alone in her struggle.* Slowly, the support that they offered her began to ground her in her convictions, and she discovered that she had not been able to confront her husband's anger and irresponsibility because of her basic fear of being emotionally alone.

She discovered that her "chickening out" was really not from a lack of conviction or backbone, but from a deep fear of making a stand and finding herself emotionally alone, without closeness to her husband. At some level, she knew that this was ridiculous, for she did not feel close to him to begin with. His behavior was interfering with the intimacy she craved, and in a deep way, she was already alone. But the conflict was more frightening than the lack of connection, and the surface, rescuing connection was better than the aloneness that she would experience when she tried to confront him.

As Debbie's connection and support increased in the group, however, she found that she could confront him and still have the support of the group. If he became enraged and did not speak to her, she would have others that cared for her and supported her. This support finally gave her the courage to make a stand. Later, when her husband finally came in for counseling, he said that the motivation to change had come when he sensed that she was finally getting strong enough that he could not control her anymore. Her strong convictions had forced him to grow up, and she could not have made those if she were not secure in other supportive relationships.

One of our most primary needs is for relationship with others, and we will often give in to compromises in values and other areas in order to have that basic need met. For that reason, good support systems are paramount in facing any difficult relationship.

2. Act righteously.

When God deals with his problem people, he acts with righteousness. He lives out his values. He practices what he preaches. In short, he always does the right thing. While this comes easily for him, however, it is difficult for us, and we would prefer that we did not have to change when we are part of the problem. Jesus, however, told us that we need to remove the log from our own eye before we can see to remove the speck from our brother's eye.

Debbie was a good example of this. As much of a problem as her husband was, the truth was that she had some weaknesses that she had to face first for the relationship to change. She had to deal with her fear of aloneness and her fear of conflict. She had to face her tendency to keep up the facade of the perfect family, hiding "family secrets" and not opening up to her friends for support and help. She had to work on communication skills to learn to deal with her husband in ways that made resolution more possible. And she had to deal with some patterns that she had from her own past that were getting in the way of healthy relating.

It would have been easier for her to avoid these painful and difficult changes in her own character, and continue to blame her husband. But our spiritual laziness never accomplishes the wish that we have for good relationships. We first have to face the ways that we are part of the problem before we can become a redemptive agent in the life of someone else. If we are still reacting to someone, we do not yet know whether or not they will or can change. We are still "returning evil for evil" (Rom. 12:17) and are still a part of the destructive pattern.

The idea of changing our own character first is really what this book is all about. In order to *have* safe people, we must first *become* safe people ourselves.

3. Use others to help.

When God is working in a person's life, he does not do it by himself—he uses the community around the problem person. He uses people to change people. In the Old Testament, he would use prophets to confront others and to discipline them. He used Nathan to confront David, and Jethro to confront Moses. He used Moses to lead and confront the people of Israel. He used his priests and teachers to discipline and guide the people that he was trying to change.

We too have a community of other believers to help us in times of need. We have others for support, as we have mentioned above. But we also have others to help us discipline people we care about. Matthew 18:15–20 tells us that when we have a difficult person to deal with and our one-on-one interventions fail, we can turn to other believers to help us in the confrontations.

This is what has been called an *intervention.* When someone difficult is not seeing that he or she has a problem, others are brought in to help in the confrontation. A problem person is more likely to listen to two or three people than one. It is easier for a problem person to defend and lie to himself with one other person than it is to several who have experienced the same problem with him. In numbers there is strength. But the guiding principle in biblical discipline is always love and humility, and it must be done by those who desire the best for the individual, not by those who are being self-righteous and punitive (see Gal. 6:1).

Loving confrontation works. Many marriages are saved because one spouse requires the other to go into counseling. People often band together to get a friend to see a counselor. Do not underestimate the power of friends or loved ones to get someone into treatment. Many of the calls that we get at our clinic are from loved ones who reach out for someone else who does not see his problem or is unable to ask for help. A good counselor can show you how to help someone else to seek help.

Finally, we use the community for wisdom and knowledge. "In an abundance of counselors there is victory" (Prov. 11:14 NASB). Often we are too caught up in the problem to see things objectively, so we need others to help us figure out the proper stance to take with the problem individual. Their input and love for the person can mitigate against our pride, hurt, and irrational behavior, as well as our own inexperience. And they can offer wise counsel to us as well as to the person with whom we are struggling.

4. Accept reality, forgive, and grieve your expectations.

Ephesians 4:32 says: "Be kind and compassionate to one another, forgiving each other, just as in Christ God forgave you."

What an incredible person to be in a relationship with! He accepts us as we are, not as he wanted us to be. This is another aspect of the way that God deals with his difficult relationships: he gave up the ideal. He gave up the wish to have a relationship with perfect people. He grieved it and decided to love us as we are. He accepted reality, because he wanted the relationship. To do that takes forgiveness and acceptance, a giving up of the way things "should be" and accepting things the way they are.

We tend to not want to do that. We do not want to give up our expectations for perfection. Instead of loving others as we find them, we want them to be different than they are, and then we will love them. We harangue each other with lists of what is wrong and what should be different, all the while missing out on the wonderful person who sits in plain view.

God did not act this way. He looked at Adam and Eve and had a choice: hold out for the ideal and miss out on them, or forgive them for not being ideal and accept them as they are. The result of the second option is that he got the relationship that he desired. Through the sacrifice of his Son, he put to rest the "should's" and accepted what was (Col. 2:13–14). As a result, we can enjoy relationship with him.

As we have seen earlier, this acceptance did not mean that he would just let things slide, not ever mentioning our faults to us again. He loves us way too much for that. But in facing problems, he is not condemning and angry. He is more interested in solving problems than shaming us or making us pay. He is not judgmental and punitive; he does not withdraw or pout when we disappoint him. He just wants to deal with things that get in the way of our relationship with him and each other, things that destroy love. He is not "nit-picky" but is interested in our well-being.

In addition to not making us feel bad for our imperfections, he is not coming to us with a list of expectations that do not fit who we are. He is not trying to change our basic personhood, from an artist to an engineer, as we sometimes try to do. He accepts who we are and tries to solve relational problems. We see couple after couple arguing not over sins, but basic personhood, demanding that the creative type they married suddenly turn into a detail-oriented person.

God made us all with different gifts for us to enjoy and to complement each other. But instead of enjoying and complementing a person's differences, accepting and even reveling in the way he is, we decide that we can do better than God and change him into something we like better. The real goal, however, should be to change *ourselves* into someone who is able to appreciate what God has created.

We need to give up our expectations for people to be faultless or to be basically different from who they really are. Maybe the person isn't so "bad" after all; maybe they are just different than we would have made them. Maybe what we are thinking is the absolute "right" way to be or to live is really a personal preference that we are trying to legislate on someone else. We tend to make our view the "right" view, even in areas where God says that other views are okay also. This is the whole concept of Christian freedom.

Before deciding to move on from a difficult relationship, make sure that you are forgiving the person for his faults. Look at yourself, to see if your own perfectionistic expectations and demands are causing the conflict. Forgive as God forgave. And appreciate the uniqueness of each individual and enjoy them, just as God enjoys us.

5. Give change a chance.

Many times people will get tired of what they have been putting up with in a relationship, and finally "get some boundaries." Then their first real exercise of boundaries will be to end the relationship. We see this often in marriage. One passive partner will get a stomach full of the other person's character problems and finally say, "Enough!" And then they will file for divorce.

They will often say that this is an exercise in "boundaries," but in reality it is a cop-out. Boundaries in a relationship are not real boundaries unless someone can exercise them in the relationship. To say that you now have boundaries, and then leave, is to not have boundaries at all.

A person with true boundaries would go back in to the relationship and take stands on the individual problems that come up within the day-to-day relationship. This is the true test of boundaries, to be in the relationship and not be controlled or abused anymore.

There are two reasons to work on boundaries within the relationship. The first is to take responsibility for one's own character. The real test of our character is to do the difficult things while in the difficult relationship, not to leave it. That is where the hard choices are. It takes a lot of courage and character to deal with a difficult person in the right way. We can only know that we have done the right thing and that we truly have character when we have been tested in the fire of relationship.

In addition, facing up to a difficult relationship is also the only guarantee that one will be able to do the right thing in a new relationship. Many times people leave one bad relationship without ever learning to do the right thing and just go repeat the cycle over again in a new one. They have not changed in the fire; they have only left the fire. That is not real change, and they are setting themselves up for failure again.

The second reason to give change a chance is that we *never really know if the relationship has a chance until we begin to do the right thing over time.* When one person changes, the relationship changes. In our experience, many difficult situations have been turned around by the character change of one party forcing change in the other. This is true in friendships, business relationships, family relationships, marriage, and dating. Therefore, before you leave a relationship, make sure that you begin to implement your changes in the relationship. Then you will know what is really there.

6. Be long-suffering.

Finally, we must remember one of the most important things that God does in his problem relationships: he is long-suffering. Exodus 34:6–7 describes God as "the compassionate and gracious God, slow to anger, abounding in love and faithfulness, maintaining love to thousands, and forgiving wickedness, rebellion and sin."

God is not someone who gives up on relationship easily. He goes the extra mile with difficult people who are important to him. And we are to model this character trait as well. He strives with humankind. He tries his best to work it out. He is not willing that any should perish, but that all would come to him and love him. And that is not a passive stance. He suffers actively and doesn't withdraw. He is "in there" trying for a long time to fix the relationship and ready to forgive when people own their part in the problem.

How long is too long? Only you and God know. But it is usually longer than we think. It is past the point of pain, past the point of revenge, past the point of despair, as he gives us the supernatural ability to love and to keep seeking an answer. That is what he did for us and that is what he calls us to do. We are to be active, going to others to work things out as best we can.

Separation: The Final Option

Finally, though, there are times when we have done all that we can do, have given it time, have opened ourselves up to trying to reconcile, and yet the person is unwilling to face his part in things. Reconciliation and change do not occur.

The Bible then tells us to separate. Matthew 18:17 tells us that after we have done all that we can do, we are to separate ourselves from the problem person until she decides to come around. In the Bible, separation is a legitimate option after all else has failed (1 Cor. 5:9–12). But even after separating we must be open to the person's later repentance and accept her back if she has truly changed (Luke 17:3–4).

The necessity of separation is a grim reality. God wishes it were not so (2 Peter 3:9); so do all of us. But the truth is that some relationships are not workable if someone is not willing to change and reconcile. We can still forgive, but we cannot reconcile without their willingness.

Jesus and Paul often said that we sometimes have to leave someone, that some relationships have to end (Matt. 10:14, 34–37; 18:17; Luke 9:59–62; Titus 3:10). But they often can be restored. For example, Paul and Barnabas disagreed over Mark, but Paul later takes him in (Acts 15:37–40; Col. 4:10). Sometimes separation is necessary, but often it is not permanent. When we separate, we are not rejecting the person; she is rejecting relationship with us. God does not send people to hell, they send themselves.

Sometimes we take a stand, and others do not accept the stand. For example, a wife takes a stand for fidelity. If her husband wants to be with her, he must remain faithful. He has a choice. She is not rejecting him if he chooses to be unfaithful; he is rejecting her values.

Remember that when we have to give up destructive relationships, we will feel a loss. Many times people try to leave a destructive relationship and do not adequately face the loss, only to find themselves going back to the same relationship or to another one just as destructive. Loss involves sadness. To have something new, however, we must first lose the old.

A Word About Divorce

Sincere Christians hold many different views about divorce. Since we are talking about when to work on a relationship and when to replace it, let us say a word here about our view on divorce and remarriage.

We think that the Bible teaches that marriage is permanent and is to be worked out. We also believe that divorce is permissible in certain circumstances—adultery or desertion by an unbelieving spouse (Matt. 5:31–32; 1 Cor. 7:15)—but God's ideal is for even those circumstances to be redeemed. That does not mean, however, that someone in a destructive, abusive situation is obliged to remain passive and be hurt.

Many times a person will remain passive until he cannot take it anymore, and then he will opt for divorce. But passivity and divorce rarely solve the problem. Dealing directly with the person in the ways described earlier give the relationship the best chance of changing. The hurting partner needs to learn how to work on her part of the relationship, and also to set appropriate boundaries against the abuse. Sometimes the hurting partner will need to separate, until the partner who is in denial sees that he needs to change. If you are in a difficult marriage, follow the steps we listed here. Get help and work on yourself, and then take the appropriate steps to influence change in the other partner. But do not passively stand by and let evil win the day.

If you are divorced, however, remember that God is a God of grace and is always willing to accept us wherever we are. He always wants to take our brokenness and start again, resurrecting what we feel is a hopeless life. If you have been divorced, he understands. He also has endured a painful divorce (Jer. 3:8), and he can help you put your life back together again.

How Long Is Long Enough?

So, when do we repair, and when do we replace? As we have seen, there is no clear-cut answer. Long-suffering is by definition long. But, in review, here are some guidelines to know when you are not ready to replace a significant relationship:

- If you are trying to resolve it alone, without the help of others
- If there are ways that you are contributing to the problem
- If you have not accepted the person as he is, forgiven him, and grieved what you wanted him to be
- If you have not gone into the relationship using new skills and responses to the difficult person, responding righteously no matter what she does
- If you have not given your new behaviors a chance to transform the relationship, seeing that redemption is a process
- If you have not been long-suffering, i.e., that the above process has continued over some time, whereby "I tried that" is a real statement, not just an excuse to check off a guilt list

These are tough requirements. They hurt, and they take time and effort on our part. But relationships are the most important aspect of the spiritual life. In fact, they *are* the spiritual life, as God defines it. To love God and love your neighbor are the main requirements of the Law.

After going through the steps we have listed, you will know that you have done all that you could. But again, be prepared. You will have to work long and hard. You will have to suffer, to change and grow. Romans 12:18 says it all: "If it is possible, as far as it depends on you, live at peace with everyone." We only know if it is possible if we have done all we can. Once we have, then we can know.

The message of this book is a lot like the message of the gospel. It has good news and bad news. The good news is that you can be saved from a life of relational hell with unsafe people. The bad news is that you must take up your cross and do the hard work of dealing with your own character problems.

We have found in our lives and in the lives of others that this process works. If you will do the hard work of distinguishing safe and unsafe people, abiding deeply with the safe ones and dealing redemptively with the unsafe ones, you will develop an abundant life, full of satisfying relationships and meaningful service to God.

Embark on a Life-Changing Journey of Personal and Spiritual Growth

Dr. Henry Cloud   *Dr. John Townsend*

Dr. Henry Cloud and Dr. John Townsend have been bringing hope and healing to millions for over two decades. They have helped people everywhere discover solutions to life's most difficult personal and relational challenges. Their material provides solid, practical answers and offers guidance in the areas of *parenting, singles issues, personal growth,* and *leadership.*

Bring either Dr. Cloud or Dr. Townsend to your church or organization.

They are available for:
- Seminars on a wide variety of topics
- Training for small group leaders
- Conferences
- Educational events
- Consulting with your organization

Other opportunities to experience Dr. Cloud and Dr. Townsend:
- Ultimate Leadership workshops—held in Southern California throughout the year
- Small group curriculum
- Seminars via Satellite
- Solutions Audio Club—Solutions is a weekly recorded presentation

For other resources, and for dates of seminars and workshops by Dr. Cloud and Dr. Townsend, visit: **www.cloudtownsend.com**

For other information **Call (800) 676-HOPE (4673)**

Or write to:
Cloud-Townsend Resources
18092 Sky Park South, Suite A
Irvine, CA 92614

Boundaries in Marriage

*Dr. Henry Cloud
and Dr. John Townsend*

Learn when to say yes and when to say no — to your spouse and to others — to make the most of your marriage.

Only when a husband and wife know and respect each other's needs, choices, and freedom can they give themselves freely and lovingly to one another. Boundaries are the "property lines" that define and protect husbands and wives as individuals. Once they are in place, a good marriage can become better, and a less-than-satisfying one can even be saved.

Drs. Henry Cloud and John Townsend, counselors and authors of the award-winning bestseller *Boundaries*, show couples how to apply the ten laws of boundaries that can make a real difference in relationships. They help husbands and wives understand the friction points or serious hurts and betrayals in their marriage — and move beyond them to the mutual care, respect, affirmation, and intimacy they both long for.

Boundaries in Marriage helps couples:

- Set and maintain personal boundaries and respect those of their spouse
- Establish values that form a godly structure and architecture for their marriage
- Protect their marriage from different kinds of "intruders"
- Work with a spouse who understands and values boundaries — or work with one who doesn't

Available in stores and online!

Boundaries with Kids

How Healthy Choices
Grow Healthy Children

Boundaries in Dating

How Healthy Choices Grow
Healthy Relationships

Our Mothers, Ourselves

How to Have That Difficult Conversation

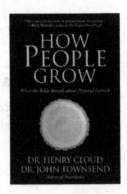